Acknowledgements

Infinite thanks and gratitude are needed for my patient boyfriend, Matthew, who supported me through the whole process.

Thanks again to Freja for her editing skills.

Thanks to everyone who bought my book on Jekyll and Hyde… it gave me the confidence to keep writing.

Finally, thanks to my mother, who was annoyed that she did not get a mention in the first book's acknowledgements. Thanks, Mum.

About the Author

Katherine holds a BA and MA in History, a PGCE in English and a 100 metre swimming certificate. She worked in schools in South London for five years, ran a school in China and now works with students who are withdrawn from mainstream education. In her spare time she runs the Straight Talking English podcast, tweets a lot, goes to vintage shops, eats Italian food and plans extravagant holidays she can't really afford.

straighttalkingenglish.com

New podcast episodes weekly on Spotify, Soundcloud, iTunes, Stitcher and Castbox.

@str8talkenglish on Twitter

Introduction

What is context?

'Context' is the background information you need to know to understand something.

Last month, I ordered poison and gave it to my boyfriend.

Am I a horrible murderer? No. I have an Amazon Prime account and we had an ant infestation, so he picked it up from the locker and used it on the patio.

You needed to know the background information to get the full meaning behind my actions and understand exactly why I am not in prison. That single idea about a relatively boring Amazon order took a whole paragraph to explain. Imagine how much stuff you need to know to understand a book written before your great-great-grandparents had lost their baby teeth! Well, if we quantified it, it'd be about a book's worth. This book, in fact!

Why should I care about context?

If you're teaching year eleven, you need to know this to fully get what your text is all about in order to get your class of little cherubs to hit AO3 in their Literature GCSEs.

If you bought this book because you just love literature, firstly: I like you. Secondly, by knowing what's swirling around the writer's head, you get a whole different perspective on the tale you're reading.

Of course, if you're in school, context is key to good grades. It's also a bonus if you get to enjoy the text you've been set, and if you know what's prompting the writer to say whatever they're saying, then it makes the story a pleasure to read.

Charles Dickens and the Power of Christmas

One fact that you, dear reader, need to know about Charles Dickens is that he loved Christmas. Putting this festival at the heart of his writing wasn't just a marketing choice, it was a way of life. Just take a look at some of his earlier journalism:

'Who can be insensible to the outpourings of good feeling, and the honest interchange of affectionate attachment, which abound at this season of the year? A Christmas family-party! We know nothing in nature more delightful! There seems a magic in the very name of Christmas. Petty jealousies and discords are forgotten; social feelings are awakened, in bosoms to which they have long been strangers; father and son, or brother and sister, who have met and passed with averted gaze, or a look of cold recognition, for months before, proffer and return the cordial embrace, and bury their past animosities in their present happiness. Kindly hearts that have yearned towards each other, but have been withheld by false notions of pride and self-dignity, are again reunited, and all is kindness and benevolence! Would that Christmas lasted the whole year through (as it ought), and that the prejudices and passions which deform our better nature, were never called into action among those to whom they should ever be strangers!'[1]

He does indeed paint a convincing picture of the power of Christmas. For many people now, Dickens and his ghost stories are the very epitome of Christmas, though other writers like Lauren Laverne disagree:

'People say Dickens invented Christmas: he didn't – though he aided its revival. Britain's newly urban population didn't have much energy or opportunity to celebrate

---

[1] Charles Dickens 'Sketches by Boz', accessed 7/19. https://ebooks.adelaide.edu.au/d/dickens/charles/d54sb/chapter34.html

it, thanks to the extremely un-festive combination of long hours of unregulated indus-
trial toil and displacement from the rural communities they'd grown up in. Dickens
was the most successful of numerous cultured Victorians keen to revive the season,
both out of nostalgia for the (more fondly than accurately) remembered country
Christmases of yore and a sense of social conscience.'[2]

Regardless of whether Charles Dickens did invent Christmas or just popularised it, the festive season as we know it fully emerged during the author's lifetime.

Obviously, Christmas had been celebrated for hundreds of years before the Victorian age, but not in a form we'd recognise today.

'Before Victoria's reign started in 1837 nobody in Britain had heard of Santa Claus
or Christmas Crackers. No Christmas cards were sent and most people did not have
holidays from work. The wealth and technologies generated by the industrial revolu-
tion of the Victorian era changed the face of Christmas forever.'[3]

The development of Christmas as an economic and cultural phenomenon is absolutely fascinating, tied in with the emergence of a distinct American culture. While Dickens was writing in London, over in the USA Washington Irving was writing a fictional travelogue about spending an old-fashioned English Christmas in the countryside. It moved him as melodramatically as Christmas moved Dickens.

[2] Lauren Laverne, 'Dickens' Christmas Carol didn't invent the holiday, but it did help revive it', accessed 7/19. https://www.theguardian.com/lifeandstyle/2014/dec/21/dickens-christmas-carol-didnt-invent-holiday-help-revived-it-lauren-laverne

[3] Ben Johnson 'A Victorian Christmas', accessed 7/19. https://www.historic-uk.com/HistoryUK/HistoryofEngland/A-Victorian-Christmas/

'It is a beautiful arrangement, also, derived from days of yore, that this festival,
which commemorates the announcement of the religion of peace and love, has been
made the season for gathering together of family connections, and drawing closer
again those bands of kindred hearts which the cares and pleasures and sorrows of the
world are continually operating to cast loose; of calling back the children of a family
who have launched forth in life, and wandered widely asunder, once more to assem-
ble about the paternal hearth, that rallying-place of the affections, there to grow
young and loving again among the endearing mementoes of childhood.

There is something in the very season of the year that gives a charm to the festivity of
Christmas. At other times we derive a great portion of our pleasures from the mere
beauties of nature. Our feelings sally forth and dissipate themselves over the sunny
landscape, and we "live abroad and everywhere." The song of the bird, the murmur of
the stream, the breathing fragrance of spring, the soft voluptuousness of summer, the
golden pomp of autumn; earth with its mantle of refreshing green, and heaven with its
deep delicious blue and its cloudy magnificence, all fill us with mute but exquisite de-
light, and we revel in the luxury of mere sensation. But in the depth of winter, when
nature lies despoiled of every charm, and wrapped in her shroud of sheeted snow, we
turn for our gratifications to moral sources. The dreariness and desolation of the
landscape, the short gloomy days and darksome nights, while they circumscribe our
wanderings, shut in our feelings also from rambling abroad, and make us more keen-
ly disposed for the pleasures of the social circle. Our thoughts are more concentrat-
ed; our friendly sympathies more aroused. We feel more sensibly the charm of each
other's society, and are brought more closely together by dependence on each other
for enjoyment. Heart calleth unto heart; and we draw our pleasures from the deep
wells of living kindness, which lie in the quiet recesses of our bosoms; and which,

when resorted to, furnish forth the pure element of domestic felicity.'⁴

The book was hugely popular on both sides of the Atlantic.

'British readers understood that it did not describe their own Christmas, but typically thought it was an accurate description of Christmases past, while American reviewers took the book as straightforward reportage'⁵

Dickens does acknowledge that the Christmas he presents in his journalism is foreign. He wrote extensively for magazines, including the one which he edited, 'Household Words'. He starts a general interest piece thusly:

'I have been looking on, this evening, at a
merry company of children assembled round
that pretty German toy, a Christmas Tree.'⁶

The Christmas that Dickens conjures in A Christmas Carol is energetically modern. Almost everything he evokes and uses as a device to provoke Scrooge's redemption had come into being within Scrooge's lifetime. Take this one particularly tender moment from Scrooge, for example:

' "What is the matter?" asked the Spirit.
"Nothing," said Scrooge. "Nothing. There was a boy singing a Christmas Carol at my door last night. I should like to have given him something: that's all." '⁷

---

⁴ Irving, Washington (2014 ed), *Old Christmas*, UK: Aristeus Books, 9.

⁵ Flanders, Judith (2017), *Christmas: A Biography*, UK: Picador, 122.

⁶ Charles Dickens, 'A Christmas Tree', accessed 7/19. http://www.djo.org.uk/household-words/volume-ii/page-289.html

⁷ Dickens, *Christmas Books,* 29.

The carol that the little boy was singing would likely have been recorded and published within five years of A Christmas Carol's publication.

'While carols were not new to the Victorians, it was a tradition that they actively re-vived and popularised. The Victorians considered carols to be a delightful form of musical entertainment, and a pleasure well worth cultivating. Old words were put to new tunes and the first significant collection of carols was published in 1833 for all to enjoy.'[8]

To return to his Christmas tree, he lists off the products that can be bought to decorate it in a kind of catalogue of items a reader could purchase from a high street.

'There were rosy-cheeked dolls, hiding behind the green leaves; there were real watches (with movable hands, at least, and an endless capacity of being wound up) dangling from innumerable twigs; there were French-polished tables, chairs, bed-steads, wardrobes, eight-day clocks, and various other articles of domestic furniture (wonderfully made, in tin, at Wolverhampton), perched among the boughs, as if in preparation for some fairy housekeeping; there were jolly, broad-faced little men, much more agreeable in appearance than many real men—and no wonder, for their heads took off, and showed them to be full of sugar-plums; there were fiddles and drums; there were tambourines, books, work-boxes, paint-boxes, sweetmeat-boxes, peep-show boxes, all kinds of boxes; there were trinkets for the elder girls, far brighter than any grown-up gold and jewels; there were baskets and pincushions in all devices; there were guns, swords, and banners; there were witches standing in en-

[8] Unknown, 'History of Christmas', accessed 7/19. http://www.bbc.co.uk/victorianchristmas/history.shtml

chanted rings of pasteboard, to tell fortunes; there were teetotums, humming-tops,

needle-cases, pen-wipers, smelling-bottles, conversation cards, bouquet-holders; real

fruit, made artificially dazzling with gold leaf; imitation apples, pears, and walnuts,

crammed with surprises; in short, as a pretty child, before me, delightedly whispered

to another pretty child, her bosom friend, "There was everything, and more." [9]

He also presents the modern Christmas in his books as one that reflects the way that people's lives worked since industrialisation had changed the world.

'Now [the festival] could be a Christmas where working people travelled home from

counting-houses and offices, where charity was the remit of the rising middle classes,

not the gentry taking care of their own tenants. Dickens took the changes to industri-

al society- office and factory work, urban poverty and want, food that was bought in

shops, not grown in kitchen-gardens, cooked in laundry -coppers and commercial

cookshops, not by servants in great halls - he took this new consumerist society, and

through Scrooge's 'conversion', turned it into a sacred duty. Following his lead -

cooking the turkey, playing games, drinking toasts, or buying a toy for your child -

became the quasi-religious observances of the new middle-class domesticity.' [10]

It's a wonderfully circular occurrence that while many credit A Christmas Carol with creating or reviving Christmas, it also represents a new kind of commodity, the book as a Christmas present. In the same way that we inevitably see the Guinness Book of Records miraculously appear every December, a cute little story book became a staple of every middle class child's Christmas stocking. Dickens deliberately produced this book and its format to appeal to

[9] Charles Dickens, 'A Christmas Tree', accessed 7/19. http://www.djo.org.uk/household-words/volume-ii/page-289.html

[10] Flanders, *Christmas*, 128.

this market, though his competitors tended to produce something more twee and saccharine.

One thing that A Christmas Carol did bring to Dickens, as well as festive cheer, was rave reviews.

''Blessings on your kind heart!' wrote Jeffrey to the author of the Carol. 'You should be happy yourself, for you may be sure you have done more good by this little publication, fostered by kindly feelings, and prompted more acts of beneficence, than can be traced to all the pulpits and confessionals since 1842.' 'Who can listen,' exclaimed Thackeray, 'to objections to a book such as this? It seems to me a national benefit, and to every man or woman who reads it a personal kindness.'[11]

An exam answer frequently read by the author during her time in the classroom was 'Dickens uses the theme of Christmas to...', and while we can say that, yes, images of Christmas are thematic to A Christmas Carol, they are representative of something else.

Christmas is used to invoke modernity and consumption, in the same way it is now. A Christmas in the twenty-first century will likely involve lots of bought gifts and time off from work, in the same way that Dickens' Christmases would. Christmas is also intrinsically linked to charity and goodwill to the poor, one of Dickens' key agendas throughout all of his work. The Christmas he invokes is also nostalgic for a pre-industrial tradition, which admittedly didn't exist, and is a reaction against how rapidly society had changed, even within his lifetime. There is no blanket image of Christmas, just a set of pictures that Dickens uses to signpost towards other issues.

---

[11] Forster, *The Life of Charles Dickens*, 345.

Christmas, as Dickens portrays it, is an intensely emotional and sentimental time. It's so easy, as readers now, to either guess at emotion or take it out of a text altogether and just look at the linguistic nuts and bolts. This is not what Dickens intended at all.

'Dickens considered it imperative for readers to experience the sensation of sentimentality in literature, rather than explain it away: this experience was moral and civilizing and designed to allow people to live harmoniously in an increasingly discordant society. While modern critics are often suspicious of this idea, it remains that civil and ethical codes in western society are still reinforced as a means for upholding good feeling between people, putting them at ease by disabling unpleasant feelings. Dickens is intent on reminding us of such codes as well as being concerned to teach us ways of reading them: he encourages us as readers to interpret the world through its emotional content, training us to do so by providing readers with literary scenes fuelled by sentimental feeling. If we then choose to critically and historically analyse these scenes, rather than experience the feeling within them, we miss their sensual expression and turn sentimentality into something else.'[12]

Christmas, for Dickens and his contemporary readers, was a sensation you are supposed to feel in your gut, as well as experience critically in your mind.

---

[12] Emma Mason, 'Feeling Dickensian Feeling', accessed 8/19. https://www.19.bbk.ac.uk/articles/10.16995/ntn.454/galley/314/download/

Ebeneezer Scrooge, Malthus and Money

'Oh! But he was a tight-fisted hand at the grindstone, Scrooge! a squeezing, wrenching, grasping, scraping, clutching, covetous, old sinner! Hard and sharp as flint, from which no steel had ever struck out generous fire; secret, and self-contained, and solitary as an oyster. The cold within him froze his old features, nipped his pointed nose, shrivelled his cheek, stiffened his gait; made his eyes red, his thin lips blue; and spoke out shrewdly in his grating voice. A frosty rime was on his head, and on his eyebrows, and his wiry chin. He carried his own low temperature always about with him; he iced his office in the dog-days; and didn't thaw it one degree at Christmas.

External heat and cold had little influence on Scrooge. No warmth could warm, no wintry weather chill him. No wind that blew was bitterer than he, no falling snow was more intent upon its purpose, no pelting rain less open to entreaty. Foul weather didn't know where to have him. The heaviest rain, and snow, and hail, and sleet, could boast of the advantage over him in only one respect. They often "came down" handsomely, and Scrooge never did.

Nobody ever stopped him in the street to say, with gladsome looks, "My dear Scrooge, how are you? When will you come to see me?" No beggars implored him to bestow a trifle, no children asked him what it was o'clock, no man or woman ever once in all his life inquired the way to such and such a place, of Scrooge. Even the blind men's dogs appeared to know him; and when they saw him coming on, would tug their owners into doorways and up courts; and then would wag their tails as though they said, "No eye at all is better than an evil eye, dark master!"

But what did Scrooge care! It was the very thing he liked. To edge his way along the crowded paths of life, warning all human sympathy to keep its distance, was what the knowing ones call "nuts" to Scrooge.'[13]

Thus, we are introduced to one of the most iconic characters in all of literature, Ebeneezer Scrooge.

What inspired Dickens to give his infamous miser this peculiar name? The short answer is insomnia and short-sightedness.

'Dickens was in the capital to deliver a lecture to an audience of Edinburgh notables. He was wandering the city, killing time before the talk, when he visited the Canongate Kirk graveyard.

There, as revealed by his diaries, he saw a memorial slab which read: "Ebenezer Lennox Scroggie - meal man". The description referred to his main trade as a corn merchant. However, the author mistakenly translated it as "mean man".'[14]

It was merely the name which Dickens chose to use in his novel rather than any information about the real Ebeneezer Scroggie, of whom historians know very little.

'Details of Scroggie's life are sparse, but he was a vintner as well as a corn merchant. He won the catering contract for the visit of George IV to Edinburgh in 1822, the first British monarch to visit since Culloden. He also secured the first contract to supply whisky to the Royal Navy.

---

[13] Dickens, Charles (1995 ed), *Christmas Books*. UK: Wordsworth Classics, 8.

[14] Unknown, 'Revealed: the Scot who inspired Dickens' Scrooge', accessed 7/19. https://www.s-cotsman.com/news-2-15012/revealed-the-scot-who-inspired-dickens-scrooge-1-571985

Scroggie was born in Kirkcaldy, Fife; his mother was the niece of Adam Smith, the
18th century political economist and philosopher.

Mr Clark added: "Scroggie was not mean-spirited, but he did attract the admonition
of the Church of Scotland by having a child out of wedlock to a servant in 1830. It is
alleged he 'ravished' her upon a gravestone. Still, what else was there to do in Edin-
burgh in 1830?" [15]

While Scroggie was somewhat free with his money, there were those who
were decidedly less inclined to spend, and misers, on the whole, were a peculiarly pre-Victorian concept, and one in particular achieved notoriety at the
time Dickens was writing. John Elwes was a three-term MP for Berkshire
who was born in 1714 to unimaginably fabulous wealth, but seemed determined not to spend a penny of it.

'Elwes would go to bed in darkness to save using a candle, and sit with his servants
in the kitchen to save lighting a fire in another room. Apart from the chill, the other
rooms in his various houses would not have been particularly nice places to sit, since
Elwes refused to pay for any maintenance. In his final years, his many homes had all
become virtually uninhabitable, though he seemed not to care, becoming of 'no fixed
abode' as he moved from one to another.

Elwes usually wore ragged clothes, going for months at a time in a single suit of
clothing that he wore in bed as well as during the day. He once spent weeks wearing
a tatty wig he found discarded in a hedge. To avoid paying for a coach Elwes would
walk in the rain, and then sit in wet clothes to save the cost of a fire to dry them. He

---

[15] Unknown, 'Revealed...'

regularly ate mouldy or putrefying food. One rumour was that he even ate a rotten moorhen he took from a rat.

Another story recounts how Elwes once badly cut both his legs while walking home in the dark, but would only allow the apothecary to treat one, wagering his fee that the untreated limb would heal first. Elwes won the bet by a fortnight, delightedly saving himself paying the doctor.

Elwes was elected MP for Berkshire in 1772, laying out just 18 pence in election expenses. His new position required regular travel to London, but he made these journeys on an emaciated horse via a roundabout route to avoid turnpike tolls. He would take along a single hardboiled egg to eat en route. After 12 years, he gave up his seat, doubtless tiring of the outrageous financial demands of being a politician. He immersed himself in full-time miserliness. On his death in 1789, he left £500,000 (almost £1bn today) to two sons born out of wedlock.'[16]

Despite giggling at the moorhen rumour, it's clear to us now that John Elwes had a psychological condition of some kind. While the real Elwes died long before Dickens' birth, his widely satirised reputation lived on, and this caricature in popular culture is likely what Dickens would have picked up on.

Like everything in the field of literature, or so it seems, Scrooge serves a symbolic purpose. Firstly, this character is a not-so-subtle dig at one of the prevailing economic theories of the time.

---

[16] Norman Miller, 'John Elwes: scrimper who inspired Ebeneezer Scrooge', accessed 7/19. https://www.telegraph.co.uk/only-in-britain/man-who-inspired-ebenezer-scrooge/

'Ebenezer Scrooge, the protagonist in Charles Dickens' A Christmas Carol, was a pitiful wretch not merely because he was miserly and misanthropic. He was also a died-in-the-wool Malthusian, telling two "portly gentlemen" raising money for charity that if the poor would rather die than go to prisons and workhouses, "they had better do it, and decrease the surplus population."'[17]

Thomas Malthus, an English clergyman, had argued as far back as 1798 in his work 'An Essay on the Principle of Population', that the earth could not support the booming population of the eighteenth century.

'Population, when unchecked, increases in a geometrical ratio. Subsistence increases only in an arithmetical ratio. A slight acquaintance with numbers will shew the immensity of the first power in comparison of the second.

By that law of our nature which makes food necessary to the life of man, the effects of these two unequal powers must be kept equal.

This implies a strong and constantly operating check on population from the difficulty of subsistence. This difficulty must fall somewhere and must necessarily be severely felt by a large portion of mankind.

Through the animal and vegetable kingdoms, nature has scattered the seeds of life abroad with the most profuse and liberal hand. She has been comparatively sparing in the room and the nourishment necessary to rear them. The germs of existence contained in this spot of earth, with ample food, and ample room to expand in, would fill

---

[17] Robert Wright 'How Charles Dickens rebukes 'overpopulation' fear mongers like Scrooge, Malthus and even today's environmentalists', accessed 7/19. https://business.financialpost.com/opinion/how-charles-dickens-rebukes-overpopulation-fearmongers-like-scrooge-malthus-and-even-todays-environmentalists

millions of worlds in the course of a few thousand years. Necessity, that imperious all pervading law of nature, restrains them within the prescribed bounds. The race of plants and the race of animals shrink under this great restrictive law. And the race of man cannot, by any efforts of reason, escape from it. Among plants and animals its effects are waste of seed, sickness, and premature death. Among mankind, misery and vice. The former, misery, is an absolutely necessary consequence of it. Vice is a highly probable consequence, and we therefore see it abundantly prevail, but it ought not, perhaps, to be called an absolutely necessary consequence. The ordeal of virtue is to resist all temptation to evil.

This natural inequality of the two powers of population and of production in the earth, and that great law of our nature which must constantly keep their effects equal, form the great difficulty that to me appears insurmountable in the way to the per-fectibility of society. All other arguments are of slight and subordinate consideration in comparison of this. I see no way by which man can escape from the weight of this law which pervades all animated nature. No fancied equality, no agrarian regulations in their utmost extent, could remove the pressure of it even for a single century. And it appears, therefore, to be decisive against the possible existence of a society, all the members of which should live in ease, happiness, and comparative leisure; and feel no anxiety about providing the means of subsistence for themselves and families.'[18]

Like so many great thinkers whose ideas have not aged well, Malthus be-lieved that it was the poor who were using up all our resources. This made them a totally unneeded section of society. Famines, war and plagues were therefore good, because they killed off the poor and left more resources for the rest of us.

---

[18] Thomas Malthus 'An Essay on the Principle of Population', accessed 7/19. https://www.guten-berg.org/files/4239/4239-h/4239-h.htm

Dickens, who had been part of this nebulous category of 'the poor', found Malthus' theories incredibly offensive and made it one of his missions to humanise the working classes as a response. Perhaps his sympathy and hope extends not only to the poor and needy, but to those who hold Scrooge's views in Stave One dear.

'Already an old man, when the story was set in the first half of the 18th century, Scrooge would have grown up before the triumph of the Smithian ideas and the repeal of the hunger-inducing, protectionist "corn laws." The psychology of the story is mixed with the economics and history of it.

Scrooge was a man whose present was distorted by his past. The old order, of monopoly and protection and tariff and hunger, gave him a nearly indelible sense of the inherent scarcity of the world. The only thing which rendered Malthus' ideas plausible to so many people was the shortage associated with command economies. Scrooge, the boy, because a victim of that, believed that want was an ontological necessity, rather than a tragic by-product of state planning.

Scrooge is not following reason; he's following trauma. His mother died when he was young. He was sent to a boarding home where he and the other children were poorly fed. By the time he was brought back from exile to his home (which his sister said is 'like heaven'), the damage to his core personality was done.

Dickens' message is clear enough: The Malthusians of his day did not need evidence (which they ignored every day in the marketplace) or reason. They needed conversion. They needed healing. They needed to be reminded on the day where the world celebrates the birth of a child whom Rome and Herod try to assign to the role of 'sur-

plus population,' that the frightened men who rule the world in the name of scarcity should not be followed, but saved.'[19]

An additional message, implicit in Stave Three, isn't that being rich is bad: it's that Scrooge is refusing to share his money by donating or spending it. Take a closer look at his description of the delicious Christmas food on offer at the market as Scrooge and the Ghost of Christmas Present walk by:

'The poulterers' shops were still half open, and the fruiterers' were radiant in their glory. There were great, round, pot-bellied baskets of chestnuts, shaped like the waistcoats of jolly old gentlemen, lolling at the doors, and tumbling out into the street in their apoplectic opulence. There were ruddy, brown-faced, broad-girthed Spanish Onions, shining in the fatness of their growth like Spanish Friars, and winking from their shelves in wanton slyness at the girls as they went by, and glanced demurely at the hung-up mistletoe. There were pears and apples, clustered high in blooming pyramids; there were bunches of grapes, made, in the shopkeepers' benevolence to dangle from conspicuous hooks, that people's mouths might water gratis as they passed; there were piles of filberts, mossy and brown, recalling, in their fragrance, ancient walks among the woods, and pleasant shufflings ankle deep through withered leaves; there were Norfolk Biffins, squat and swarthy, setting off the yellow of the oranges and lemons, and, in the great compactness of their juicy persons, urgently entreating and beseeching to be carried home in paper bags and eaten after dinner. The very gold and silver fish, set forth among these choice fruits in a bowl, though members of a dull and stagnant-blooded race, appeared to know that there was something

---

[19] Jerry Bowyer, 'Malthus and Scrooge: How Charles Dickens Put Holly Branch Through the Heart Of The Worst Economics Ever', accessed 7/19. https://www.forbes.com/sites/jerrybowyer/2012/12/24/malthus-and-scrooge-how-charles-dickens-put-holly-branch-through-the-heart-of-the-worst-economics-ever/#11e92134672d

going on; and, to a fish, went gasping round and round their little world in slow and

passionless excitement.

The Grocers'! oh, the Grocers'! nearly closed, with perhaps two shutters down, or

one; but through those gaps such glimpses! It was not alone that the scales descend-

ing on the counter made a merry sound, or that the twine and roller parted company

so briskly, or that the canisters were rattled up and down like juggling tricks, or even

that the blended scents of tea and coffee were so grateful to the nose, or even that the

raisins were so plentiful and rare, the almonds so extremely white, the sticks of cin-

namon so long and straight, the other spices so delicious, the candied fruits so caked

and spotted with molten sugar as to make the coldest lookers-on feel faint and subse-

quently bilious. Nor was it that the figs were moist and pulpy, or that the French

plums blushed in modest tartness from their highly-decorated boxes, or that every-

thing was good to eat and in its Christmas dress; but the customers were all so hur-

ried and so eager in the hopeful promise of the day, that they tumbled up against each

other at the door, crashing their wicker baskets wildly, and left their purchases upon

the counter, and came running back to fetch them, and committed hundreds of the like

mistakes, in the best humour possible; while the Grocer and his people were so frank

and fresh that the polished hearts with which they fastened their aprons behind might

have been their own, worn outside for general inspection, and for Christmas daws to

peck at if they chose.'[20]

The fact that Dickens devotes a significant amount of space to this description shows the importance he places on it, tempting us as much as it does
Scrooge.

---

[20] Dickens, *Christmas Books*, 46.

'[T]he ghost raises his torch (in the shape of a cornucopia) and leads Scrooge to the public market, brimming with food from all around the world. Dickens especially emphasizes the fruits of trade: almonds, Spanish onions and oranges (in winter, no less). The message is clear: Use your eyes, man, just look around and see that the dirge-ists of the day are wrong. England, even with its poor classes, is a prosperous society. The world is abundant. Rest is possible. So is generosity.'[21]

To go a step deeper, it's not merely generosity that Scrooge is learning about: it's how to be a good consumer and participate economically in the 'right' way. Lyn Pykett clarifies:

'In his miserly mode, Scrooge has sought to acquire money rather than the goods it can buy, and to impose on others his own lack of desire for our pleasure in consumption. Scrooge's redemption or progress consists of his learning how to be a good consumer, and how to keep money and goods in (benevolent) circulation.'[22]

However, Edmund Wilson's landmark 1942 essay on Dickens entitled 'The Two Scrooges' offers a different perspective on Scrooge that doesn't revolve around his economic status.

'We have come to take Scrooge so much for granted that he seems practically a piece of Christmas folklore; we no more inquire seriously into the mechanics of his transformation than we do into the transformation of the Beast into the young prince that marries Beauty in the fairy tale. Yet Scrooge represents a principle fundamental to the dynamics of Dickens' world and derived from his own emotional constitution—

---

[21] Bowyer, 'Malthus and Scrooge'.

[22] Pykett, Lyn (2002), *Critical Issues: Charles Dickens*, UK: Palgrave, 94.

though the story, of course, owes its power to the fact that most of us feel ourselves capable of the extremes of both malignity and benevolence.'[23]

Dickens especially fell into this camp, as he could be both a warm and loving father and a cruel and cold man who could easily block people out of his life.

'This dualism runs all through Dickens. There always has to be a good and a bad of everything: each of the books has its counterbalancing values, and pairs of characters sometimes counterbalance from different books.'[24]

It became a preoccupation to try and write characters who were both good and bad rather than falling into only one category. It's tempting to see this as Dickens' way to reconcile the different sides of his character: the lavish literary celebrity, the perpetually broke businessman, the kind friend and the angry control freak. Scrooge is his prototype of a flawed character who raises questions about sympathy and blame, and who we grow to like. Wilson is far less optimistic, however.

'Shall we ask what Scrooge would actually be like if we were to follow him beyond the frame of the story? Unquestionably he would relapse when the merriment was over—if not while it was still going on—into moroseness, vindictiveness, suspicion. He would, that is to say, reveal himself the victim of a manic-depressive cycle, and a very uncomfortable person.'[25]

---

[23] Edmund Wilson, 'The Two Scrooges', accessed 7/19. https://newrepublic.com/article/100447/the-two-scrooges

[24] Wilson 'The Two Scrooges'.

[25] Wilson 'The Two Scrooges'.

Charles Dickens was very concerned about his own finances at the time of writing. He'd negotiated a weird agreement with his publishers where, if enough books sold he would make a profit, and if sales were too low he owed them money. Sadly, while his way of distributing his books by sending out a chapter a week by subscription was hugely successful, his latest book, Martin Chuzzlewit, was sold in a single volume and that wasn't what the people wanted. He was in the middle of trying to break his contract with his publishers while writing A Christmas Carol, so money was on his mind. He decided to work with his publishers one last time to try and make a profit on a desirably festive item. His friend and biographer, Forster, was nervous:

'He had entrusted the Carol for publication on his own account, under the usual terms of commission, to the firm he had been so long associated with; and at such a moment to tell them, short of absolute necessity, his intention to quit them altogether, I thought a needless putting in peril of the little book's chances. He yielded to this argument; but the issue, as will be found, was less fortunate than I hoped.'[26]

Dicken's hunch that the Carol would be a success was absolutely spot on, and six thousand copies were bought on the first day of its release. By the start of January, thousands more had been ordered by bookshops. Alas, he'd made an accounting error: unlike his normal magazine-style chapters, A Christmas Carol was published as a beautiful colour book that was expensive to make, and he'd set the price very low. He aimed to make a thousand pounds from the publication of A Christmas Carol,[27] but sadly had only made £230 after the initial run, by which time he needed to pay his former publisher[28]. Dickens felt himself to be on the brink of ruin. Luckily, when he

---

[26] Forster, *Charles Dickens*, 333.

[27] £67,000 today.

[28] £15,000 today.

switched publisher, he received a generous advance and as more copies of the Carol sold, he found himself far more financially comfortable.

Bob Cratchit and the Poor

Bob Cratchit, the experts feel, is mostly based on Dickens' own father, drawing on these lines as evidence:

'*The office was closed in a twinkling, and the clerk, with the long ends of his white comforter dangling below his waist (for he boasted no great-coat), went down a slide on Cornhill, at the end of a lane of boys, twenty times, in honour of its being Christmas Eve, and then ran home to Camden Town as hard as he could pelt, to play at blindman's-buff.*'[29]

Upon moving to London, Dickens and his family lived in a small and slightly run-down house in Camden. John Dickens also has a cameo in David Copperfield as Mr Micawber:

'*The only visitors I ever saw, or heard of, were creditors. THEY used to come at all hours, and some of them were quite ferocious. One dirty-faced man, I think he was a boot-maker, used to edge himself into the passage as early as seven o'clock in the morning, and call up the stairs to Mr. Micawber— 'Come! You ain't out yet, you know. Pay us, will you? Don't hide, you know; that's mean. I wouldn't be mean if I was you. Pay us, will you? You just pay us, d'ye hear? Come!' Receiving no answer to these taunts, he would mount in his wrath to the words 'swindlers' and 'robbers'; and these being ineffectual too, would sometimes go to the extremity of crossing the street, and roaring up at the windows of the second floor, where he knew Mr. Micawber was. At these times, Mr. Micawber would be transported with grief and mortification, even to the length (as I was once made aware by a scream from his wife) of making motions at himself with a razor; but within half-an-hour afterwards, he would polish up his*

---

[29] Dickens, *Christmas Books,* 15.

26

shoes with extraordinary pains, and go out, humming a tune with a greater air of

gentility than ever.'[30]

Sadly, John Dickens' contribution to history has mostly been fuelling his son's interest in helping the poor. John came from a working class background, the son of two servants, and rose up the ranks of the administrative arm of the Navy to occupy a respected and well-paying position. Unfortunately, he lived dramatically beyond his means and accrued debts he couldn't pay, leading him to debtors' prison.[31] Biographer Claire Tomalin characterises John Dickens in more friendly terms:

'John Dickens was expansive by nature, with a tendency to speak in loose, grand

terms, and an easy way with money. When required to describe himself he wrote

'gentleman' on documents and announced himself as 'Esquire' in the newspaper an-

nouncement of his first son's birth. He liked to dress well, as young Regency bucks

did, he bought expensive books and enjoyed entertaining friends, from whom he

might later ask for a loan.'[32]

Regardless of his father's lack of prudence with money and his later tendency to look for handouts from his son, Charles always remembered the family's Christmases in reduced circumstances very fondly. He later recounted:

'I know my father to be as kind hearted and as generous a man as ever lived in the

world. Everything I can remember of his conduct to his wife, or children, or friends,

in sickness or affliction, is beyond all praise. By me, as a sick child, he has watched

---

[30] Charles Dickens, 'Great Expectations', accessed 7/19. https://www.gutenberg.org/files/766/766-h/766-h.htm

[31] More on this later...

[32] Tomalin, Claire (2011), *Charles Dickens: A Life.* UK: Penguin, 7.

night and day, unweariedly and patient, many nights and days. He never undertook any business, charge or trust that he did not zealously, conscientiously, punctually, honourably discharge.'[33]

The Cratchit family home is directly based on the Dickens family home at this point in his life. His best friend and biographer, John Forster, recalled:

'Bayham Street was about the poorest part of the London suburbs then and the house was a mean, small tenement, with a wretched little back garden abutting on a squalid court. Here was no place for new acquaintances for him: no boys were near with whom he might hope to become in any way familiar. A washerwoman lived next door, and a Bow-Street Officer[34] lived over the way. Many, many times he had spoken to me of this, and how he seemed at once to fall into a solitary condition apart from all the boys of his own age, and to sink into a neglected state at home which has always been quite unaccountable to him . . . That he took, from the very beginning of this Bayham Street life, his first impression of the struggling poverty which is nowhere more vividly shown than in the commoner streets of the ordinary London suburb.'[35]

The Cratchits also play into Dickens' anti-Malthus agenda:

'To the modern eye, the Cratchit family is no paragon of "zero population growth" — the Malthusian dictum popularized in the 1970s that sought to limit children to two per couple. The Cratchits have six kids, whom they plainly love beyond measure but struggle to support (Dickens himself had 10). The most cherished of the Cratchit

---

[33] Devito, Carlo (2014), *Inventing Scrooge: The Incredible True Story Behind Dickens' Legendary A Christmas Carol.* Maine: Cider Mill Press, 86.

[34] Policeman.

[35] Devito, *Inventing Scrooge*, 80.

brood is the disabled Tiny Tim, whose survival is by no means assured. Dickens may have intuited that if Malthusian principles were ever harnessed to the project of actually culling the human herd, the disabled would be the first to go.'[36]

In fact, by Stave Two, we know that the Cratchits are not poor and hungry because there is a lack of resources: it's completely due to Scrooge's decision to pay Bob Cratchit a pittance.[37]

'For three full paragraphs, he describes in mouth-watering detail the seemingly limitless variety and sumptuousness of the foods available to Londoners. "Heaped up on the floor," we read, "were turkeys, geese, game, poultry, cherry-cheeked apples, juicy oranges, luscious pears, immense twelfth-cakes, and seething bowls of punch." Surrounded by such abundance, the ghost reveals to Scrooge two pitiful waifs, symbolizing ignorance and want. And just to drive home the disparity, he whisks Scrooge off to the home of his own clerk, Bob Cratchit, to reveal how little of London's bounty will grace the Cratchit Christmas — the result not of Malthusian scarcity but rather of the pitiful wages paid by Scrooge.'[38]

Bob and his family are symbolic of the 'deserving poor': those who work hard but cannot make ends meet, as opposed to those who were seen as 'undeserving' because they were beggars or resorted to crime. Bob Cratchit is literate, as are his sons, and his daughter has a respectable job as an apprentice. They are an idealised poor family, and reflect Dickens' agenda to humanise the working class and present them sympathetically. In fact, when Mrs Cratchit expresses a dislike for Scrooge, we as readers find ourselves on

---

[36] Wright, 'How Charles Dickens rebukes...'

[37] Though, ironically, the fifteen shillings Bob receives is the going rate for his services, the emotional equivalent of paying someone minimum wage today.

[38] Wright, 'How Charles Dickens rebukes...'

her side, which seems an unusual position if we were contemporary middle class readers.

'"Mr. Scrooge!" said Bob; "I'll give you Mr. Scrooge, the Founder of the Feast!"

"The Founder of the Feast indeed!" cried Mrs. Cratchit, reddening. "I wish I had him here. I'd give him a piece of my mind to feast upon, and I hope he'd have a good appetite for it."

"My dear," said Bob, "the children! Christmas Day."

"It should be Christmas Day, I am sure," said she, "on which one drinks the health of such an odious, stingy, hard, unfeeling man as Mr. Scrooge. You know he is, Robert! Nobody knows it better than you do, poor fellow!"

"My dear," was Bob's mild answer, "Christmas Day."

"I'll drink his health for your sake and the Day's," said Mrs. Cratchit, "not for his. Long life to him! A merry Christmas and a happy new year! He'll be very merry and very happy, I have no doubt!"

The children drank the toast after her. It was the first of their proceedings which had no heartiness. Tiny Tim drank it last of all, but he didn't care twopence for it. Scrooge was the Ogre of the family. The mention of his name cast a dark shadow on the party, which was not dispelled for full five minutes.'[39]

But what of the poor who Scrooge refuses to help, namely those who the 'portly gentlemen' were collecting for? They would face a shameful fate: that of the workhouse.

'The provision of state-provided poor relief was crystallised in the 1601 Poor Relief Act, which gave parish officials the legal ability to collect money from rate payers to spend on poor relief for the sick, elderly and infirm – the 'deserving' poor. Labelled

---

[39] Dickens, *Christmas Books*, 35.

'out relief', handouts usually took the form of bread, clothing, fuel or money.

Though they were termed 'workhouses' from the 1620s, the early institutions that provided poor relief were, more often than not, non-residential, offering handouts in return for work. Much like today's taxpayers, those funding poor relief were anxious to see their money well spent, wishing to deter those capable of working from claiming assistance. By the end of the 17th century, providing care under one roof was widely regarded as the most effective way of saving money and, as a result, the early 1700s saw a flurry of workhouses opening.

Yet workhouses only really became part of Britain's social landscape after 1723, when Sir Edward Knatchbull's Workhouse Test Act won parliamentary approval. The act embodied the principle that the prospect of the workhouse should act as a deterrent and that relief should only be available to those desperate enough to accept its regime. Its impact on the provision of poor relief was dramatic: by the 1770s the number of parish workhouses in England and Wales had soared to around 2,000.

Conditions during the early 19th century, though, meant the government was forced to reassess the way it helped the most impoverished members of society. The return of unemployed or injured servicemen from the Napoleonic Wars saw the national poor relief bill quadruple between 1795 and 1815, rising from £2 million to £8 million. To make matters worse, new Corn Laws restricted grain imports and pushed up the cost of bread.

The government's response was to pass a Poor Law Amendment Act in 1834, based on the recommendation of a royal commission. The new system was still funded by rate payers, but was now administered by unions – groupings of parishes – presided over by a locally elected Board of Guardians. Each union was responsible for providing a central workhouse for its member parishes, and out relief was abolished except in special cases. For the able-bodied poor, it was the workhouse or nothing.'[40]

To go to the workhouse was incredibly shameful, and Scrooge is essentially suggesting that he only considers the poor as objects rather than people with feelings. Dickens had a mission against these places, as shown by his article in Household Words (the magazine he also ran):

'A melancholy case of Death from Starvation, has occurred at Southampton. Elizabeth Biggs, a delicate young woman, whose poverty had made her a constant recipient of parish relief for some months past, applied one day, towards the end of last month, to the parish doctor for medical relief. He saw that she was more in need of nourishment and shelter than of medicines, and he gave her an order for immediate admission to the workhouse. Her brother accompanied her thither, and she obtained admission; but it would seem that she remained only a short time. Too delicate to endure the severe cold of the lodging in the "tramp-house," where casual paupers are given shelter for the night on a bed of straw, with the covering of one quilt, she complained of illness, and, on her own request, was let out of the workhouse. She was found by her sister in the afternoon, sitting on the ground in the street, with her child of two years old at her side; she seemed too weak to go on to the lodging-house on which she had a poor-law order for a night's sleep. Her sister took her to this lodging-house for the night. Next day her sister found her very ill indeed, from sheer starvation; and asked why she had not applied to the workhouse people for a loaf. "A tall man, a doctor," she said, "told the relieving-officer not to do so; and bade her go to her own parish, for her parish would not do so for them." Her sister persuaded her to

---

[40] Charlotte Hodgman, 'The Rise and Fall of the Workhouse', accessed 7/19. https://www.histo-ryextra.com/period/victorian/the-rise-and-fall-of-the-workhouse/

go once more to the workhouse; but the porter refused admittance, on the ground that
she had no order for that day. The sister took her to lodgings, and paid for a bed for
one more night.

Next at Manchester. Mary Hunter, a woman who gained a scanty livelihood by selling
apples, &c., was taken ill with pain in her side on Saturday week. She lodged in the
kitchen of Mrs. M'Donough, a woman nearly as poor as herself, and slept on the
flagged floor, with but a few flocks between her and the stones, and a piece of carpet
for her sole covering; she was corpulent, however, and did not while well suffer
acutely from cold. Mrs. M'Donough went for a medical man several times that day,
but could not get one. On Sunday, the 30th ult., she got directions to put on a poul-
tice; which was put on, without relief to the patient. On Monday the poor woman was
dangerously ill, and consented that an order for the workhouse should be applied for;
but Mr. Pierce, the relieving-officer, had moved his residence and could not be found
for some time: he gave a note to Mr. Noble, the parish doctor; and the note was de-
livered, but "no one came that day." On Tuesday, Mr. Noble's assistant, Mr. Brown,
came, and ordered a poultice; but said nothing about removal of the patient from the
stone floor. He directed Mrs. M'Donough to come for medicine; she went, and was
told she must fetch a bottle—no bottle would be given with the medicine; after further
loss of time a bottle was got, and the medicine procured and administered—without
relief. During Tuesday more poultices—without effect; more messages backwards and
forwards to the relieving-officer and surgeon, with warnings that the woman would
be dead by morning. Visits were made by the officer and surgeon late in the evening.
On Wednesday the poor woman grew worse, and on Thursday morning she died. On
a post-mortem examination, it appeared that she died of acute internal inflammation;
and Mr. George Morley Harrison, surgeon, deposed that such a condition would, in
the first instance, be produced by exposure to cold, and would subsequently be ag-

33

gravated by the want of proper nourishment and other comforts. The Coroner's Jury returned a verdict of "Died from inflammation of the lungs, aggravated by exposure and lying in the place deserted;" and they expressed their unanimous opinion that there had been neglect on the part of the overseer and the medical man who visited the deceased; recommending that a copy of the depositions be forwarded to the Poor-law Board.

A third case of a similar kind has been discovered in the Metropolis. On the 1st inst., an inquest was held respecting the death of a middle-aged man who had Died from Want and Exposure to the Cold. It appeared that on the previous Friday morning, Mrs. Gibbs, residing in Tyndall Buildings, Gray's-inn Lane, was alarmed by hearing some person moaning in the cellar of the house, and found the deceased lying in a corner of the cellar, huddled up in a quantity of filth and dirt. He was insensible, and Mrs. Gibbs immediately obtained the assistance of several police-constables, who had him removed to Holborn workhouse. He was stripped and placed in hot blankets, and the usual remedies of ammonia and brandy were applied; but he never rallied, and died shortly afterwards. Two penny-pieces were found placed upon two ulcers on his legs, and a few pieces of stale bread were also discovered in his pockets. He had obtained admission to the cellar by the window which looked into the street. The coroner remarked that the cellar appeared to be in the same bad condition as before the cholera broke out; and that the parochial authorities ought to have the place thoroughly cleansed every week. The Jury returned a verdict of— "Death from exhaustion, caused by exposure to the cold, and the want of the common necessaries of life." [41]

---

[41] Charles Dickens, 'Accident and Disaster', accessed 8/19. http://www.djo.org.uk/household-narrative-of-current-events/year-1850/page-11.html

While this might be included in the news section of Household Words, this is clearly Dickens picking the most tragic cases he could to draw his readers' attention to the situation of the poor.

The portly gentlemen and their role is very interesting since we, as twenty-first century people, know of the existence of organised charities and may well support several ourselves. This was a very recent idea for Dickens' readers:

'The nineteenth century, with its spectacular growth in the number of voluntary organizations, was undoubtedly a great philanthropic age. A letter to the editor of The Times, in 1884, reflected upon the 'immense ocean of charity' at work in the metropolis. Indeed, the periodical The Philanthropist suggested that the metropolis could be better named 'Philanthropis'. Various charitable directories, such as The Classified Directory to the Metropolitan Charities and Herbert Fry's Royal Guide to the London Charities, detailed the millions of pounds raised annually by charities at work in metropolis. The Times, in reporting this fact, asserted that the income of these London charities was greater than the national budgets of the Swiss Confederation, Denmark, Portugal and Sweden. Whether or not this claim was true, it is certain that charity was a pervasive force in the nineteenth century.' [42]

Not only is Scrooge rejecting the chance to be nice, he is rejecting the opportunity to be modern and participate in society. He has the opportunity to remain anonymous if he doesn't feel comfortable doing so in public, and yet he still refuses. The kind-hearted souls of London would immediately see that Scrooge is not a pleasant character, making his transformation even more miraculous.

---

[42] Sarah Flew, 'Unveiling the anonymous philanthropist: charity in the nineteenth century', accessed 8/19. http://eprints.lse.ac.uk/61080/1/Flew_Unveiling_the_Anonymous_Philanthropist.pdf

In contrast to the miserable Scrooge, look at the sheer happiness and activity with which Dickens describes the Cratchit's dinner:

'Such a bustle ensued that you might have thought a goose the rarest of all birds; a feathered phenomenon, to which a black swan was a matter of course — and in truth it was something very like it in that house. Mrs. Cratchit made the gravy (ready before-hand in a little saucepan) hissing hot; Master Peter mashed the potatoes with incred-ible vigour; Miss Belinda sweetened up the apple-sauce; Martha dusted the hot plates; Bob took Tiny Tim beside him in a tiny corner at the table; the two young Cratchits set chairs for everybody, not forgetting themselves, and mounting guard upon their posts, crammed spoons into their mouths, lest they should shriek for goose before their turn came to be helped. At last the dishes were set on, and grace was said. It was succeeded by a breathless pause, as Mrs. Cratchit, looking slowly all along the carving-knife, prepared to plunge it in the breast; but when she did, and when the long expected gush of stuffing issued forth, one murmur of delight arose all round the board, and even Tiny Tim, excited by the two young Cratchits, beat on the table with the handle of his knife, and feebly cried Hurrah!

There never was such a goose. Bob said he didn't believe there ever was such a goose cooked. Its tenderness and flavour, size and cheapness, were the themes of universal admiration. Eked out by apple-sauce and mashed potatoes, it was a sufficient dinner for the whole family; indeed, as Mrs. Cratchit said with great delight (surveying one small atom of a bone upon the dish), they hadn't ate it all at last! Yet every one had had enough, and the youngest Cratchits in particular, were steeped in sage and onion to the eyebrows! But now, the plates being changed by Miss Belinda, Mrs. Cratchit

*left the room alone—too nervous to bear witnesses—to take the pudding up and bring
it in.*

*Suppose it should not be done enough! Suppose it should break in turning out! Sup-
pose somebody should have got over the wall of the back-yard, and stolen it, while
they were merry with the goose—a supposition at which the two young Cratchits became livid! All sorts of horrors were supposed.*

*Hallo! A great deal of steam! The pudding was out of the copper. A smell like a wash-
ing-day! That was the cloth. A smell like an eating-house and a pastrycook's next
door to each other, with a laundress's next door to that! That was the pudding! In half
a minute Mrs. Cratchit entered—flushed, but smiling proudly—with the pudding, like
a speckled cannon-ball, so hard and firm, blazing in half of half-a-quartern of ignited
brandy, and bedight with Christmas holly stuck into the top.*
*Oh, a wonderful pudding! Bob Cratchit said, and calmly too, that he regarded it as
the greatest success achieved by Mrs. Cratchit since their marriage. Mrs. Cratchit
said that now the weight was off her mind, she would confess she had had her doubts
about the quantity of flour. Everybody had something to say about it, but nobody said
or thought it was at all a small pudding for a large family. It would have been flat
heresy to do so. Any Cratchit would have blushed to hint at such a thing.'[43]*

The bustling joy Dickens shares with us gives the reader such a quick impression of the value of the poor family's nostalgic Christmas that we can't
help but like them, and the juxtaposition of hinting at the level of their poverty
mixes this appeal with sympathy for them. Even in the nicest bits of this novel, Dickens is still playing with the middle class reader's heartstrings.

---

[43] Dickens, *Christmas Books*, 55.

Tiny Tim and Illness

'Alas for Tiny Tim, he bore a little crutch, and had his limbs supported by an iron frame!' [44]

Poor Tiny Tim was designed to raise sympathy from the reader as much as from Scrooge. His adorable cry of 'God Bless Us, Everyone!' is deliberately crafted to pull on the heartstrings and raise the sentimentality of this book as high as it will go.

Was there a real Tiny Tim? Actually, there were two. One of them was Dickens' own nephew, Henry Burnett Jr,[45] who was the son of his favourite sister, Fanny.

'Fanny's crippled eldest son, who always had a fragile hold on life, seemed unlikely to outlive his mother by much, if at all.' [46]

This boy also apparently had a habit of saying things that were incredibly mature for his age, and it's easy to picture Dickens being entranced by a little lad waxing lyrical on the power of Christmas while celebrating himself.

Through a lot of research, we can work out which illness inflicts Tiny Tim: a combination of rickets and tuberculosis.

---

[44] Dickens, *Christmas Books*, 34.

[45] He was also the model for Paul Dombey on Dickens' later work 'Dombey and Son'.

[46] Devito, *Inventing Scrooge*, 143.

'Rickets is a deficiency disease caused by a lack of minerals in the bones. In the 1800s the disease was widespread in the poor districts of industrial cities in Great Britain and the United States.

Minerals are used to strengthen bones - without them bones become soft and bent. The symptoms of rickets usually started showing in young children who grew up with twisted and bent limbs. The body needs vitamins and sunlight to be able to absorb minerals into the skeleton. Therefore, rickets was particularly common among the poor, whose diet did not provide enough vitamins, and among people who did not get a lot of sunlight.'[47]

If Scrooge did indeed take a parental role in raising Tiny Tim, as is implied at the very end of Stave Five, then with enough nutritious food and sunlight, Tiny Tim would indeed grow up to be a healthy young man, despite this affliction.

The TB that Tiny Tim also suffered from was a whole different issue, however.

'Today we know tuberculosis is an infectious disease caused by the bacterium Mycobacterium tuberculosis. At the beginning of the 19th century, however, physicians were still in doubt as to whether it was an infectious disease, a hereditary condition or a type of cancer. Indeed, it was only in 1865 that a French military doctor demonstrated that the disease could be passed from humans to cattle, and from cattle to rabbits. This was a remarkable breakthrough. Until this time, medical theory held that each case of consumption arose spontaneously in predisposed people.

[47] Unknown, 'Rickets', accessed 7/19. http://broughttolife.sciencemuseum.org.uk/broughttolife/techniques/rickets

In the UK and Europe, consumption caused the most widespread public concern during the 19th and early 20th centuries. It was seen as an endemic disease of the urban poor. By 1815 it was the cause of one in four deaths in England, up from 20% in 17th century London. In Europe, rates of tuberculosis began to rise in the early 1600s and peaked in the 1800s when it also accounted for nearly 25% of all deaths. Between 1851 and 1910 in England and Wales four million died from consumption, more than one-third of those aged 15 to 34 and half of those aged 20 to 24, giving consumption the name the robber of youth.

When a person is infected with Mycobacterium tuberculosis, they are unlikely to display any immediate symptoms. Patients with a healthy immune system, good nutrition and clean air are often able to overcome the disease. Even without treatment, approximately 20% of those who contract the disease can make a full recovery.

Consumption, however, was closely linked to both overcrowding and malnutrition making it one of the principal diseases of poverty. In the 19th century, when many of the lower classes lived in crowded, unsanitary conditions, with weakened immune systems brought on by poor nutrition and ill health, it is easy to see how an untreatable condition such as consumption could take hold. In 1838 and 1839, in England, between a quarter and a third of tradesmen and labourers died from tuberculosis. The figure was approximately one-sixth in "gentlemen".

Wealthy tuberculosis sufferers could afford to travel in search of sunny and mild climates, whereas poorer people had to look after their own ill consumptive family. Often in dark, unventilated, closed rooms, they sealed their own fate to die of the same disease a few years later.'[48]

I choose to believe that with a few trips to the countryside and the best medical care Scrooge could offer, Tiny Tim would survive this too, but given the state of pollution in London and his living conditions, sadly Tiny Tim may not have survived this one.

While deeply moving to us now, it was sadly a common occurrence for a Victorian family to lose a child.

'No one was immune. The great scientist, Charles Darwin, lost his 10-year-old daughter, Annie [left], to tuberculosis in 1851. In his personal memoir, the grief-stricken father wrote: 'We have lost the joy of the household, and the solace of our old age...Oh that she could now know how deeply, how tenderly we do still & and shall ever love her dear joyous face.' By the mid-19th century, tuberculosis accounted for as many as 60,000 children's deaths per year.'[49]

Readers from all over the UK, rich and poor, loved Dickens' books, and many of them could have lost children or siblings, making the image of the empty chair and crutch a sadly personal reminder of their own lives. The scale to which his readership was affected is difficult to judge, however, and greatly depended on where they were from or living. Since Dickens' appeal was almost universal, it's safe to assume that many were.

Including a disabled character is a bold move for a nineteenth century Dickens, but a reasonable one considering his agenda to humanise outsiders. He

[48] VL McBeath, 'Consumption: The Most Feared Of Diseases', accessed 7/19. https://valmcbeath.com/consumption-the-most-feared-of-diseases/

[49] Dr Lindsey Fitzharris, 'Death and Childhood in Victorian England', accessed 7/19 http://www.dr-lindseyfitzharris.com/2013/10/15/death-childhood-in-victorian-england/

would pick up this theme of highlighting disadvantaged children throughout his work, such of in Nicholas Nickleby:

'Pale and haggard faces, lank and bony figures, children with the countenances of old men, deformities with irons upon their limbs, boys of stunted growth, and others whose long meagre legs would hardly bear their stooping bodies, all crowded on the view together; there were the bleared eye, the hare-lip, the crooked foot, and every ugliness or distortion that told of unnatural aversion conceived by parents for their offspring, or of young lives which, from the earliest dawn of infancy, had been one horrible endurance of cruelty and neglect. There were little faces which should have been handsome, darkened with the scowl of sullen, dogged suffering; there was childhood with the light of its eye quenched, its beauty gone, and its helplessness alone remaining; there were vicious faced boys, brooding, with leaden eyes, like malefactors in a jail; and there were young creatures on whom the sins of their frail parents had descended, weeping even for the mercenary nurses they had known, and lonesome even in their loneliness. With every kindly sympathy and affection blasted in its birth, with every young and healthy feeling flogged and starved down, with every revengeful passion that can fester in swollen hearts, eating its evil way to their core in silence, what an incipient Hell was breeding here!'[50]

Now, looking critically at Tiny Tim, he could be written off as a token character, were it not for the role he and others like him would play in the development of charity.

The dependent person with a disability - especially the child- was able to awaken the heart of Economic Man (Scrooge) and soften the iron laws of economics. Though the laws cannot be abrogated, charitable feelings can be exercised outside their sphere.

---

[50] Quoted in Diniejko, 'Charles Dickens as Social Commentator and Critic'.

Public philanthropy directed towards those who fall out of the economic equation is the secular version of longstanding Christian charitable imperatives directed towards the poor and helpless in general. The dependent person with a disability - Tiny Tim - has no independent character in his drama. In this tale, there is no possibility that a person with a disability might be able to have an independent economic function if adaptations are made. Nor does Tiny Tim have the option of refusing the charity he inspires.'[51]

It is a conundrum for someone looking at nineteenth century charity and disability: are these efforts denying someone like Tiny Tim their own active life if they're forced to take them? Is Dickens just encouraging the rich to act for the poor and take over their lives? I am inclined to think not. Dickens' London residence[52] is incredibly close the first charitable home opened by Thomas Barnardo, and his philosophy differed greatly from that suggested above.

'[In] Victorian London's East End, where Thomas Barnardo set up his first home for boys in 1870, there was. . . post-Industrial Revolution overcrowding, filth, poverty and disease to contend with. Poor children suffered from rickets, curved spines, respiratory diseases, inherited syphilis and a variety of deformities.

But Barnardo prided himself on welcoming children of all abilities and health into his care. In 1877, he wrote: "Given the destitution and when accompanied by disease, deformity or ill-health…. We will render assistance."

He disapproved of segregation between abled and disabled children, declaring in-

---

[51] Devito, *Inventing Scrooge*, 146.

[52] Now the Charles Dickens Museum.

43

stead that all young people could benefit from integration. "Unkindness to these little unfortunates from the other boys or girls," he wrote, "is a thing quite unknown to us."

Barnardo believed that "the presence of a child maimed for life, or marked by some serious deformity, draws out only kind deeds and gentle thoughts from the roughest boys and wildest girls".

Knowing the reality of the world around them, however, he also made sure disabled children learnt marketable trades. The boys practised tailoring; the girls learnt embroidery. At Barnardo's school for deaf, blind and disabled girls in Hackney, the children also wove Persian rugs, sewed tapestries and hand-painted lace.'[53]

With Tiny Tim as the ultimate sympathetic character, Dickens created a relatable image of a child that appealed to people based on their own experiences with mortality, and lent a human face to progressive charitable movements.

But what of the other two ill children, largely ignored by busy teachers and those who want the whimsical aspects of the story: Ignorance and Want, symbolically conjured by The Ghost of Christmas Present.

'The chimes were ringing the three quarters past eleven at that moment.

---

[53] Harriet Marsden, 'Disability History Month: Barnardos publishes 125-year-old photos of disabled children', accessed 7/19. https://www.independent.co.uk/arts-entertainment/photography/disability-history-month-barnardos-photos-disabled-children-kids-differently-abled-handicapped-a8071336.html

"Forgive me if I am not justified in what I ask," said Scrooge, looking intently at the Spirit's robe, "but I see something strange, and not belonging to yourself, protruding from your skirts. Is it a foot or a claw?"

"It might be a claw, for the flesh there is upon it," was the Spirit's sorrowful reply.

"Look here."

From the foldings of its robe, it brought two children; wretched, abject, frightful, hideous, miserable. They knelt down at its feet, and clung upon the outside of its garment.

"Oh, Man! look here. Look, look, down here!" exclaimed the Ghost.

They were a boy and girl. Yellow, meagre, ragged, scowling, wolfish; but prostrate, too, in their humility. Where graceful youth should have filled their features out, and touched them with its freshest tints, a stale and shrivelled hand, like that of age, had pinched, and twisted them, and pulled them into shreds. Where angels might have sat enthroned, devils lurked, and glared out menacing. No change, no degradation, no perversion of humanity, in any grade, through all the mysteries of wonderful creation, has monsters half so horrible and dread.

Scrooge started back, appalled. Having them shown to him in this way, he tried to say they were fine children, but the words choked themselves, rather than be parties to a lie of such enormous magnitude.

"Spirit! are they yours?" Scrooge could say no more.

"They are Man's," said the Spirit, looking down upon them. "And they cling to me, appealing from their fathers. This boy is Ignorance. This girl is Want. Beware them both, and all of their degree, but most of all beware this boy, for on his brow I see that written which is Doom, unless the writing be erased. Deny it!" cried the Spirit, stretching out its hand towards the city. "Slander those who tell it ye! Admit it for your factious purposes, and make it worse. And bide the end!"

"Have they no refuge or resource?" cried Scrooge.

"Are there no prisons?" said the Spirit, turning on him for the last time with his own words. "Are there no workhouses?"

The bell struck twelve.'[54]

Dickens has put us as readers in Scrooge's place, and turned the blame towards us as part of society. He also has given a glaring image that Victorian readers can relate to, but has flown over the modern day reader's head. The image is hunger. We've all been hungry at one point or another, but persistent and long term deprivation and hunger was part and parcel of an average Victorian life. The historian Ruth Goodman notes that:

'For many Victorians, food was permanently and exclusively on their mind, and they could do nothing but watch the effects of hunger reap damage on their families, powerless to prevent it . . .chronic lifelong nutritional stress must have been the day to day experience of many. The self control and self denial induced by hunger were thought to teach enduring habits of self-sacrifice and aid fashioning a more moral in-

---

[54] Dickens, *Christmas Books*, 45.

dividual.'[55]

The inclusion of these children has two functions. Firstly, if a poorer reader is desperately hungry, they could see themselves in these characters and see how the rich should feel sympathy for them. The rich, themselves perhaps part of this general acceptance that less food is fine, could see what they had created in this horrific portrayal of two children.

Food is a key symbol in A Christmas Carol, according to Dickensian scholar Lydia Craig:

'Dickens's extensive meat imagery acts as a doling-out measure for how much meat should be allotted to each person regardless of their financial status. Considering that the repeal of the ban against importing meat from Europe, specifically beef and pork, had been enacted the previous year under Sir Robert Peel's administration. . .

Just prior to Dickens's writing of A Christmas Carol in October of 1843, an increase in the price of meat due to poor manufactures had resulted in low consumption of meat in England from 1842 through the early part of 1843. Taken in conjunction with the Corn Laws (1815-1846), which imposed restrictions on the import of grain, higher meat prices meant that while the nation's butchering capacity should have allowed for a ratio of 122 lbs. of cow and hog meat per individual, the poor were forced to largely go without this food source, exacerbating their impoverished situation. While the Corn Laws temporarily remained in effect, the prohibition against the importation of animals was lifted on July 9, 1842, requiring an import duty of twenty shillings a head on oxen and bulls, fifteen shillings on cows, three shillings on sheep, five on hogs, etc. According to John Ramsay McCulloch writing in June 1843 on the subject

---

[55] Goodman, Ruth (2013), *How to be a Victorian*, UK: Penguin, 172.

of "Cattle" for A Dictionary, Practical, Theoretical, and Historical of Commerce and
Commercial Navigation, the repeal "certainly was one of the most important inroads
that has ever been made on the prohibitive system, and reflects the greatest credit on
the administration of Sir Robert Peel". However, McCulloch expressed doubt con-
cerning the measure's effectiveness, observing, "The benefits of the measure are
rather of a prospective and negative than of an immediate and positive description...
it will no doubt prevent or be a great obstruction to any oppressive rise in future in
the price of butcher's meat in this country; but we doubt whether it will do more than
this". While lamenting Parliament's refusal to allow the importation of corn, he does
welcome the move as a check against price inflation: "Though the new measure
should not lower the price of butcher's meat, it will, at all events, prevent its farther
increase, and enable provision to be made for the wants of our rapidly increasing
population". By bringing Scrooge to the recognition of his own duty to provide the
poor with meat on Christmas Day in a year in which its price skyrocketed, Dickens
makes a political argument for the holiday as a permanent, social state of mind, ad-
vocating charity's role in bridging the wide gap between the different foods available
to the rich and to the disadvantaged.

Consciously, Dickens equates human bodies with the bodies of animals, which,
through being subsumed into hungry stomachs, can potentially confer physical vigor
and alertness impossible to achieve otherwise. Audrey Jaffe has noted, "The story's
most famous icon, Tiny Tim, figures sympathy in an economy of representation and
consumption. Scrooge's macabre remark that the Cratchits' Christmas turkey is
'twice the size of Tiny Tim' associates such plenitude with the object of sympathy in a
manner that has become paradigmatic for A Christmas Carol itself". Coming as it
does in Stave 5, this remark of Scrooge's reflects his final acceptance of the ghosts'
didactic message and resolution to fill empty, ailing bodies with plenitude. In Stave 1,

when asked by two charitable (and portly) gentlemen "to buy the Poor some meat and drink and means of warmth," Scrooge refuses. After Thomas Malthus, Scrooge instead famously advocates death by starvation as a necessary measure to "decrease the surplus population". As scathing as Dickens can be towards the wealthy who withhold sustenance and basic comforts of life from the poor, he also critiques those who also deny themselves. Though Scrooge could easily purchase meat for himself and others, part of the close-fisted meanness of his character is his willingness to deny himself meat, crouching over gruel to combat his cold instead of something heartier like beef-tea.'[56]

[56] Lydia Craig 'Man and Meat: A Christmas Carol's Cannibalistic Menace in Historical Perspective', accessed 8/19. http://dickenssociety.org/?p=1535

Women and Domesticity

It's well known, to the point of being a cliché, that Dickens couldn't write female characters well. The women who inhabit his books are generally two-dimensional and seem to be sentimental window-dressing at best. Take Fred's wife, for example:

'She was very pretty: exceedingly pretty. With a dimpled, surprised-looking, capital face; a ripe little mouth, that seemed made to be kissed—as no doubt it was; all kinds of good little dots about her chin, that melted into one another when she laughed; and the sunniest pair of eyes you ever saw in any little creature's head. Altogether she was what you would have called provoking, you know; but satisfactory, too. Oh, perfectly satisfactory.'

We know that she's happy and likes to laugh, but her personality? No chance of mentioning that. In this respect, Dickens tends to follow the conventional ideas of the time on how a woman should present herself, and focuses only on this idealised picture of women, such as this one shown in a father's advice to his daughters:

'One of the chief beauties in a female character, is that modest reserve, that retiring delicacy, which avoids the public eye, and is disconcerted even at the gaze of admiration.—I do not wish you to be insensible to applause. If you were, you must become, if not worse, at least less amiable women. But you may be dazzled by that admiration which yet rejoices your hearts.

When a girl ceases to blush, she has lost the most powerful charm of beauty. That extreme sensibility which it indicates may be a weakness and incumbrance in our sex, as I have too often felt; but in yours it is peculiarly engaging. Pedants, who think themselves philosophers, ask why a woman should blush when she is conscious of no crime? It is a sufficient answer, that nature has made you to blush when you are guilty of no fault, and has forced us to love you because you do so.—Blushing is so far from being necessarily an attendant on guilt, that it is the usual companion of innocence.

This modesty, which I think so essential in your sex, will naturally dispose you to be rather silent in company, especially in a large one.—People of sense and discernment will never mistake such silence for dulness. One may take a share in conversation without uttering a syllable. The expression in the countenance shows it, and this never escapes an observing eye.'[57]

Perhaps the most influential description of a Victorian woman is in Coventry Patmore's incredibly popular poem 'The Angel in the House', published in 1854, loudly proclaiming the virtues of a lovely submissive and domestic wife.

'Man must be pleased; but him to please
Is woman's pleasure; down the gulf
Of his condoled necessities
She casts her best, she flings herself.
How often flings for nought, and yokes
Her heart to an icicle or whim,
Whose each impatient word provokes
Another, not from her, but him;
While she, too gentle even to force

---

[57] John Gregory 'A Father's Legacy to his Daughters', accessed 7/19. https://www.gutenberg.org/files/50108/50108-h/50108-h.htm#conduct

His penitence by kind replies,

Waits by, expecting his remorse,

With pardon in her pitying eyes;

And if he once, by shame oppress'd,

A comfortable word confers,

She leans and weeps against his breast,

And seems to think the sin was hers;

Or any eye to see her charms,

At any time, she's still his wife,

Dearly devoted to his arms;

She loves with love that cannot tire;

And when, ah woe, she loves alone,

Through passionate duty love springs higher,

As grass grows taller round a stone.'[58]

Somewhat nauseating reading today, it also connects to Dickens' own wife, Catherine. On the rebound, Dickens chose to marry his own 'Angel In the House' as the lovely Catherine appealed to him after he had been dumped by a fiery and independent girl.

'She was not clever or accomplished like his sister Fanny and could never be his in-tellectual equal, which may have been part of her charm: foolish little women are more often presented as sexually desirable in his writing than clever competent ones. He wanted to be married. He did not want a wife who would compel his imagination.'[59]

---

[58] Coventry Patmore 'The Angel in The House', accessed 7/19.
http://academic.brooklyn.cuny.edu/english/melani/novel_19c/thackeray/angel.html

[59] Tomalin, *Dickens*, 57.

Together they had ten children and a relatively happy relationship, for a while at least.

Domestic settings pop up throughout Dickens' work, and serve to create a contrast between the home and whatever it is he is critiquing, and the women he writes about fit into that vision too. To a certain extent he is a product of his time, however:

'The characterisation of the home as an enclave of family warmth and harmony and its superintendence by a woman who embodies the domestic ideal are key elements in the ideology of the middle class family.'[60]

Dickens was, of course, firmly middle class by this point in his career, and the Christmases he celebrated with his family are warm, cosy celebrations too, as his daughter later described:

'On Christmas Day we all had our glasses filled, and then my father, raising his, would say: "Here's to us all. God bless us!", a toast which was rapidly and willingly drunk. His conversation, as may be imagined, was often extremely humorous, and I have seen the servants, who were waiting at table, convulsed often with laughter at his droll remarks and stories. Now, as I recall these gatherings, my sight grows blurred with the tears that rise to my eyes. But I love to remember them, and to see, if only in memory, my father at his own table, surrounded by his family and friends - a beautiful Christmas spirit.'[61]

---

[60] Jordan, John O (ed, 2001), *The Cambridge Companion to Charles Dickens*, UK: Cambridge, 121.

[61] Dickens, Mamie (2011 edition), *My Father as I Recall Him*, USA: Library of Alexandria, 13.

The domestic Christmases in his books don't just serve to amuse the characters, however.

'Dickens draws a contrast between such cozy homes, which harbour the domestic ideal, and great houses . . . which are inhabited by alienated or embittered occupants'[62]

The only other house we as readers have been inside is Scrooge's, and it's the polar opposite of the adorable Cratchit house. He is the outsider now, despite the fact he should be well included into Victorian society, and Dickens uses this setting to (once again) show how isolated Scrooge is and how miserable he has become despite his wealth.

Not only is he lonely, but he's also implicitly morally bad as he's single. It's noted in present day scholarship that:

'possession of the ideal middle class home (suitably superintended by the Angel in the House) becomes the sign of moral virtue and guarantor of male identity'[63]

Without this kind of a home and wife, Scrooge is devoid of any kind of identity at all. This is where Mrs Cratchit comes in: despite her occasional sassiness, her role as the loving housewife shows that the Cratchit family are morally 'correct', hammering home the idea that Scrooge is wrong. She is indeed the 'Angel in the House' that makes the Cratchits seem perfect.

"The mother laid her work upon the table, and put her hand up to her face.
"The colour hurts my eyes," she said.

---

[62] Jordan, *The Cambridge Companion*, 123.

[63] Jordan, *The Cambridge Companion*, 124

The colour? Ah, poor Tiny Tim!

"They're better now again," said Cratchit's wife. "It makes them weak by candle-light; and I wouldn't show weak eyes to your father when he comes home, for the world. It must be near his time."

"Past it rather," Peter answered, shutting up his book. "But I think he has walked a little slower than he used, these few last evenings, mother."

They were very quiet again. At last she said, and in a steady, cheerful voice, that only faltered once:

"I have known him walk with—I have known him walk with Tiny Tim upon his shoulder, very fast indeed."

"And so have I," cried Peter. "Often."

"And so have I," exclaimed another. So had all.

"But he was very light to carry," she resumed, intent upon her work, "and his father loved him so, that it was no trouble: no trouble. And there is your father at the door!"

She hurried out to meet him; and little Bob in his comforter—he had need of it, poor fellow—came in. ''[64]

Of course, Dickens would soon be outside this domestic setting by 1858, slightly over eleven years after A Christmas Carol was written. In classic sit-com style, a gorgeous bracelet intended to be delivered to an eighteen year old woman[65] he fancied, Nelly Ternan, was accidentally delivered to his wife. After an understandably huge fight, they separated. Dickens took the unusual step of pre-empting any rumours by publishing a statement on the front page of his magazine, Household Words:

---

[64] Dickens, *Christmas Books*, 62.

[65] Dickens was 45 at this point.

'Dickens tells his readers: "Some domestic trouble of mine, of long-standing [has]
lately been brought to an arrangement which involves no anger or ill-will." Dickens
also denounces the rumors linking him either with his wife's sister, Georgina, or with
the young actress, Ellen Ternan. The always indiscreet Thackeray, when told Dickens
was having an affair with Georgina, blurted, "Oh, no, it's with an actress!" The New
York Times had written that Dickens and his paramour had eloped to Boulogne. La-
beling the allegations, "most grossly false, most monstrous and most cruel," Dickens
concludes, "Whosoever repeats one of them after this denial, will lie as wilfully and
fouly as it is possible for any false witness to lie, before Heaven and earth."

Intimates of the author knew of his domestic difficulties - and his relationship with
Miss Ternan - but had urged a quiet separation. Dickens would not listen, "A dismal
failure has to be borne, and there is an end." In a letter to his American publisher,
soon printed in England, Dickens referred to Catherine's "peculiarities of character"
and "mental disorders," concluding "We are in all respects... wonderfully unsuited to
each other."' [66]

Yet, despite this behaviour, Dickens was still seen as the ultimate perfect
celebrity.

'Dickens wished to be, and was, generally worshipped - the word is not too strong for
a person who evoked comparison with Christ at the time of his death - as a man of
unblemished character , the incarnation of broad christian virtue and at the same
time of domestic harmony and conviviality. The jolly domestic part of his reputation
had been acquired young, through his early novels and his notably exuberant and

[66] Tom Hughes, 'An Announcement from Mr Dickens', accessed 8/19. http://victoriancalen-dar.blogspot.com/2011/06/june-12-1858.html

hospitable family life; it had been crowned by his Christmas stories and never dis-lodged.'[67]

This image, which was sustained after Dickens' separation, is what makes his presentation of domestic life so fascinating. He wrote descriptions of the home life he imagined he could have experienced as boy, intermingled with his experiences of married life. This image he created outlived his own experiences and became a key part of the Dickens myth that we know today.

A discussion of relationships past and future would not be complete without an inspection of Belle, Scrooge's ex-fiancée.

'For again Scrooge saw himself. He was older now; a man in the prime of life. His face had not the harsh and rigid lines of later years; but it had begun to wear the signs of care and avarice. There was an eager, greedy, restless motion in the eye, which showed the passion that had taken root, and where the shadow of the growing tree would fall.

He was not alone, but sat by the side of a fair young girl in a mourning-dress: in whose eyes there were tears, which sparkled in the light that shone out of the Ghost of Christmas Past.

"It matters little," she said, softly. "To you, very little. Another idol has displaced me; and if it can cheer and comfort you in time to come, as I would have tried to do, I have no just cause to grieve."

"What Idol has displaced you?" he rejoined.

"A golden one."

[67] Tomalin, Claire (1990), *The Invisible Woman: The Story of Nellie Ternan and Charles Dickens*, UK: Penguin, 4.

"This is the even-handed dealing of the world!" he said. *"There is nothing on which it is so hard as poverty; and there is nothing it professes to condemn with such severity as the pursuit of wealth!"*

"You fear the world too much," she answered, gently. *"All your other hopes have merged into the hope of being beyond the chance of its sordid reproach. I have seen your nobler aspirations fall off one by one, until the master-passion, Gain, engrosses you. Have I not?"*

"What then?" he retorted. *"Even if I have grown so much wiser, what then? I am not changed towards you."*

She shook her head.

"Am I?"

"Our contract is an old one. It was made when we were both poor and content to be so, until, in good season, we could improve our worldly fortune by our patient industry. You are changed. When it was made, you were another man."

"I was a boy," he said impatiently.

"Your own feeling tells you that you were not what you are," she returned. *"I am. That which promised happiness when we were one in heart, is fraught with misery now that we are two. How often and how keenly I have thought of this, I will not say. It is enough that I have thought of it, and can release you."*

"Have I ever sought release?"

"In words. No. Never."

"In what, then?"

"In a changed nature; in an altered spirit; in another atmosphere of life; another Hope as its great end. In everything that made my love of any worth or value in your sight. If this had never been between us," said the girl, looking mildly, but with steadiness, upon him; *"tell me, would you seek me out and try to win me now? Ah, no!"*

58

He seemed to yield to the justice of this supposition, in spite of himself. But he said

with a struggle, "You think not."

"I would gladly think otherwise if I could," she answered, "Heaven knows!

When I have learned a Truth like this, I know how strong and irresistible it must be.

But if you were free to-day, to-morrow, yesterday, can even I believe that you would

choose a dowerless girl—you who, in your very confidence with her, weigh everything

by Gain: or, choosing her, if for a moment you were false enough to your one guiding

principle to do so, do I not know that your repentance and regret would surely fol-

low? I do; and I release you. With a full heart, for the love of him you once were."

He was about to speak; but with her head turned from him, she resumed.

"You may—the memory of what is past half makes me hope you will—have pain in

this. A very, very brief time, and you will dismiss the recollection of it, gladly, as an

unprofitable dream, from which it happened well that you awoke. May you be happy

in the life you have chosen!"

She left him, and they parted.'[68]

Again, this is a part of the book that does not translate well into the twenty-first century world. A dowry was an amount of money given to the groom by the bride's family when a couple became engaged. It was a tradition dating back thousands of years, and while it's easy to say that Belle dumps Scrooge because she can't provide any money, the issue goes deeper than that.

'The size of the dowry was expected to be in direct proportion to the groom's social

status, thus making it virtually impossible for lower class women to marry into upper

class families.

---

[68] Dickens, *Christmas Books*, 42.

If a woman's family was too poor to afford a dowry, the economic circumstance may have been forbidden her from ever marrying. One of her few options might be to become a mistress to a richer man who could afford to support a large household. Or, sometimes wealthy parishioners might provide dowries for poor young women of good reputation as a form of charity. Overall, dowries were a significant consideration for the marriage opportunities of a daughter, and for the marriage choices of a young gentleman.'[69]

It isn't just that Belle won't have the money available to help Scrooge become set up in life, it's that she will drag him down socially. His position as a member of the middle class is too important to him, and Belle knows that to marry her would cause him shame since she would now be considered 'poor'. The fact she is portrayed in a mourning dress might be Dickens doing a bit of subtle foreshadowing, or it might signify that she has not received an inheritance. Either way, she is doomed to be classified as the working class, and knows the rules of society well enough to break off her engagement. Of course, the third option alluded top above would be Scrooge's mistress, but Belle is smart enough to know that if she has sex with Scrooge outside of marriage, she could be considered an irredeemable fallen woman.

Belle reappears later in the stave, looking a lot happier:

'They were in another scene and place; a room, not very large or handsome, but full of comfort. Near to the winter fire sat a beautiful young girl, so like that last that Scrooge believed it was the same, until he saw her, now a comely matron, sitting opposite her daughter. The noise in this room was perfectly tumultuous, for there were more children there, than Scrooge in his agitated state of mind could count; and, un-

[69] Allyson Thaxton, 'Married to Money: Dowries in Victorian England', accessed 8/19. https://byuprideandprejudice.wordpress.com/2014/02/03/married-to-money-dowries-in-victorian-england/

like the celebrated herd in the poem, they were not forty children conducting them-
selves like one, but every child was conducting itself like forty. The consequences
were uproarious beyond belief; but no one seemed to care; on the contrary, the moth-
er and daughter laughed heartily, and enjoyed it very much; and the latter, soon be-
ginning to mingle in the sports, got pillaged by the young brigands most ruthlessly.
What would I not have given to be one of them! Though I never could have been so
rude, no, no! I wouldn't for the wealth of all the world have crushed that braided
hair, and torn it down; and for the precious little shoe, I wouldn't have plucked it off,
God bless my soul! to save my life. As to measuring her waist in sport, as they did,
bold young brood, I couldn't have done it; I should have expected my arm to have
grown round it for a punishment, and never come straight again. And yet I should
have dearly liked, I own, to have touched her lips; to have questioned her, that she
might have opened them; to have looked upon the lashes of her downcast eyes, and
never raised a blush; to have let loose waves of hair, an inch of which would be a
keepsake beyond price: in short, I should have liked, I do confess, to have had the
lightest licence of a child, and yet to have been man enough to know its value.

But now a knocking at the door was heard, and such a rush immediately ensued that
she with laughing face and plundered dress was borne towards it the centre of a
flushed and boisterous group, just in time to greet the father, who came home attend-
ed by a man laden with Christmas toys and presents. Then the shouting and the
struggling, and the onslaught that was made on the defenceless porter! The scaling
him with chairs for ladders to dive into his pockets, despoil him of brown-paper
parcels, hold on tight by his cravat, hug him round his neck, pommel his back, and
kick his legs in irrepressible affection! The shouts of wonder and delight with which
the development of every package was received! The terrible announcement that the
baby had been taken in the act of putting a doll's frying-pan into his mouth, and was

61

more than suspected of having swallowed a fictitious turkey, glued on a wooden plat-
ter! The immense relief of finding this a false alarm! The joy, and gratitude, and ec-
stasy! They are all indescribable alike. It is enough that by degrees the children and
their emotions got out of the parlour, and by one stair at a time, up to the top of the
house; where they went to bed, and so subsided.'[70]

By no means is Belle wealthy, but despite her lack of wealth she is very happy. This is what begins to hurt Scrooge as he sees that he could have been happy with her without money, and that she is doing very well for herself without the dowry which had so much importance placed on it. This is the character whose appearance begins to thaw the icy Scrooge.

What of the real female readers that bought Dickens' books? They may well have empathised with the portly gentlemen, since charity was very much a woman's concern.

'Free from the cut and thrust of commercial life and widely thought to be more sensi-
tive than men to suffering and personal relations, women were increasingly called
upon to be agents of social improvement. "In charity", as a writer in the English
Woman's Journal put it, "there will always be found a congenial sphere for the
fruition of the unemployed energies of women". Like medieval churchmen who fell
back on morality to increase their power in a society dominated by an armed aristoc-
racy, nineteenth-century women exploited the belief in their superior morality to in-
crease their power in a society dominated by men.

By the mid-nineteenth century the range of women's activities was enormous, and
through determination, ingenious fundraising, and a willingness to take on work that

---

[70] Dickens, *Christmas Books*, 45.

62

men were unwilling or unable to do, they had broken down much of the prejudice against them in the charitable establishment.

While it is impossible to be precise about their overall financial contribution to philanthropy in the nineteenth century, women dramatically increased their share of charitable funding. In a growing number of societies they provided the bulk of the income. In the Royal Society for the Prevention of Cruelty to Animals (RSPCA), for example, women made up 69% of the subscribers by 1900, and their financial contribution was roughly in line with that figure. Increasingly prominent in the world of organised philanthropy, they began to redirect the nation's charitable energies into channels that suited their perception of society's needs, most notably causes associated with the welfare of women and children. In district visiting, for example, the forerunner of social work, women became so ubiquitous that commentators often used the pronoun 'she' when referring to visitors.

As the influence of women in charity increased it whetted their appetite for more, and a larger and larger number of institutions emerged with women in charge. In 1893, The Englishwoman's Yearbook estimated that there were about 500,000 women who laboured "continuously and semi-professionally" in philanthropy and another 20,000 who supported themselves as "paid officials" in charitable societies.

With the years women extended their activities to campaigns for legal and moral reform. Many charitable campaigners joined the women's suffrage societies, which some saw as part of the wider moral reform movement. Charitable work provided a variety of experience, not least in administration, that was a very useful introduction to other professions. As a religion of action philanthropy challenged the complacency of women, gave them practical responsibility, and heightened their self-confidence

63

and self esteem.'[71]

Scrooge's alienation of the charity collectors therefore would be likely to annoy many in his female readership. In order to get this female readership, however, it had to make his books appropriate for women, at least according to Victorian standards.

'Dickens's novels date from the 1830s to 1870, when women were legally the property of their husbands, fathers or whichever male relative called themselves "head of the family". His heroines, including Flora Finching, Dora Spenlow and Rosa Budd – described in The Mystery of Edwin Drood as "wonderfully pretty, wonderfully childish" – are often infuriating to read now. At the time of their creation, however, Dickens was emulating a popular impression of what a well-brought up young lady should be like.

Many Victorian girls and even adult women were forbidden by their families to read novels if the heroines were considered too controversial (including Anne Brontë's The Tenant of Wildfell Hall and Charlotte Brontë's Jane Eyre). Instead they were recommended to read "improving" books, often written by religious writers, about how girls and women should behave: think Jessica's First Prayer by Hesba Stretton and Coventry Patmore's narrative poem The Angel in the House. Queen Victoria famously sacked her daughters' governess after discovering one of the princesses reading a novel.'[72]

---

[71] Frank Prochaska, 'Women and philanthropy in nineteenth century England', accessed 8/19. http://www.philanthropy-impact.org/article/women-and-philanthropy-19th-century-england

[72] Lucinda Dickens Hawksley, 'Charles Dickens and the women who made him', accessed 8/19. https://www.theguardian.com/books/2016/apr/06/charles-dickens-and-the-women-who-made-him

Dickens, ever the hustling publicist, needed to balance the demands of those who bought the books, and his own personal views. Women did definitely read his books, so this gamble must have worked out for him!

'An elderly charwoman employed about the place had shown so much sympathy in the family trouble, that Mrs. Hogarth especially told her of the approaching visit, and who it was that was coming to the sick-room. "Lawk ma'am!" she said. "Is the young gentleman upstairs the son of the man that put together Dombey?" Reassured upon this point, she explained her question by declaring that she never thought there was a man that could have put together Dombey. Being pressed farther as to what her notion was of this mystery of a Dombey (for it was known that she could not read), it turned out that she lodged at a snuff-shop kept by a person named Douglas, where there were several other lodgers; and that on the first Monday of every month there was a Tea, and the landlord read the month's number of Dombey, those only of the lodgers who subscribed to the tea partaking of that luxury, but all having the benefit of the reading; and the impression produced on the old charwoman revealed itself in the remark with which she closed her account of it. "Lawk, ma'am! I thought that three or four men must have put together Dombey!" [73]

As with the entire Christmas Carol project, Dickens wanted a book which would make money and fit into then-current trends, and Belle and Mrs Cratchit definitely served this purpose.

Jacob Marley and Punishment

The scary arrival of Scrooge's old business partner heralds the turn of the novel towards a supernatural direction. It also features another name that Dickens had taken from his life, as historian Barry West discovered in 2017:

[73] E D H Johnson, 'Dickens and His Readers', accessed 8/19. http://www.victorianweb.org/authors/dickens/edh/3.html

'"I was sent a newspaper clipping from the Dickens expert, which said that on St Patrick's Day, at 11 Cork Street, Westminster, London, a Dr Miles Marley had invited guests over to celebrate – one of those guests was Charles Dickens.

"The clipping said that Dickens had started a discussion over unusual names and it was agreed that Marley was indeed an unusual name. It was said that Dickens told Marley, 'by the end of the year your name will be a household word'." [74]

To embrace the Cornish connection further, Dickens' train to visit his friends would have passed through the Marley Tunnel, and it's easy to imagine the daydreaming writer picking up on this name.

The scholar Carlo Devito also believes that Dickens' choice to use the first name Jacob could be a biblical reference.

'The biblical story of Jacob is told in the Book of Genesis. The story 'Jacob's Ladder' is named after his vision of a ladder that climbs to heaven and provides escape for the Israelites. After being estranged from his mother, father and brother, Jacob returns to his homeland seeking reconciliation, especially with his brother, Esau. He was alone at that time, hoping to find peace with God the night before their family's reunion. That night, in the dark, he wrestled with what he thought was a man until the break of day. As the light of dawn broke, and Jacob could see the shadow he'd been wrestling with all night, Jacob insisted the man bestow a blessing on him. The

---

[74] Nicola Slawson, 'Charles Dickens' A Christmas Carol' inspired by visits to Cornwall', accessed 7/19. https://www.theguardian.com/books/2017/dec/19/charles-dickens-a-christmas-carol-inspired-by-visits-to-cornwall

*'man' revealed himself to be an angel of God. The angel then blessed Jacob and
gave him the name 'Israel' (Yisrael), meaning 'the one who wrestled with God"[75]*

While this interpretation of Marley as some kind of personified divine interven-
tion is interesting, it falls flat when we consider the fact that Dickens was not
a particularly religious man.

*'In all his writings, Charles Dickens—a Christian of the broadest kind—is outspoken
in his dislike of evangelicalism and Roman Catholicism, but, especially in his fiction,
he is very reluctant to make professions of a specific faith beyond the most general
sort of Christianity. Nothing more surely aroused his suspicions about a person's religious faith than a public profession of it, and this aversion formed a fundamental
feature of his dislike of evangelicals and dissenters.'[76]*

That said, other current writers disagree, arguing that the biblical imagery in A
Christmas Carol is far too blatant to ignore.

*'Christian theology leaps off the pages of "A Christmas Carol" and is the essence of
Dickens. As the late Eleanor Farjeon wrote in a 1954 introduction to "A Christmas
Carol," "To separate the feast of Dickens from the festival of Christ would do Boz
poor justice," Boz being the pen name used by Dickens in his earliest works.*

*Christian theology is so essential to the Dickens Christmas that the celebration is not
just of the saga between Nativity and Epiphany. The Dickens Christmas celebrates
the entire story of Christ, from Nativity to the Resurrection. For instance, in "The*

---

[75] Devito, *The Invention of Scrooge,* 89.

[76] Unknown, 'What were Charles Dickens' views toward religion?', accessed 7/19. https://dicken-s.ucsc.edu/resources/faq/religion.html

Christmas Tree" (the first of Dickens' "Christmas Stories") the author lists every biblical event in the life of Christ as part of Christmas. And in "What Christmas Is As We Get Older" (the second of Dickens' "Christmas Stories") the author cites the adult Christ raising the daughter of Jairus from the dead as part of the Christmas story.

Nowhere in the works of Dickens is Christian theology more obvious than in "A Christmas Carol." Hardly secular concepts, the tale contains the twin themes of redemption and forgiveness. Paul Davis wrote in his 1990 book, "The Lives and Times of Ebenezer Scrooge," that Scrooge's odyssey is a journey from the Old Testament to the New Testament.

The allegory is most compelling when considering the three nights of Scrooge's ordeal. Remember that it is only in the movies where Scrooge's experience with the Christmas ghosts all takes place on Christmas Eve. In the actual tale written by Dickens, Scrooge's conversion at the hands of the ghosts takes place over the course of three nights. It is only by the miracle of the Christmas Ghosts of Past, Present, and Yet to Come that Scrooge is able to wake on Christmas morning after three nights having passed since Christmas Eve. And these three nights of Scrooge's ordeal are representative of Christ rising on the third day.

But the Christian theology of "A Christmas Carol" is not limited to allegory. Indeed, most of the theological symptoms are explicit and concrete. Most memorable are the words of Tiny Tim, the afflicted son of Scrooge's beleaguered clerk Bob Cratchit, who tells his father on their way home from church that he hoped people had seen him with his crutch so as "to remember on Christmas Day who made lame beggars walk and blind men see."

There is also the example of Scrooge's nephew Fred, who sings the praises of Christmas "apart from the veneration due its sacred name and origin, if anything belonging to it can be apart from that, as a good time." This passage brings us back to Eleanor Farjeon's point that the feast of Dickens is inseparable from the festival of Christ.

Lest we forget, there is also the passage when Scrooge is visited by the two charitable gentlemen soliciting funds "to make some slight provision for the poor and destitute." In response to Scrooge's insensitive suggestion that the poor and destitute belong in prisons and workhouses, one of the gentleman replies that prisons and work-houses "scarcely furnish Christian cheer of mind or body to the multitude."

Nor can we forget the ghost of Scrooge's late partner Jacob Marley who laments "Not to know that any Christian spirit will find its mortal life too short for its vast means of usefulness." Marley's ghost goes on to lament never having raised his eyes "to that blessed star which led the Wise Men to a poor abode."

There is also the author himself interjecting his Christian theology. He instructs the reader that it is good to be child-like at Christmas "when its mighty founder was a child himself." [77]

The most obvious feature of the ghostly Marley when he appears in Stave One is that he is imprisoned.

'The same face: the very same. Marley in his pigtail, usual waistcoat, tights and boots; the tassels on the latter bristling, like his pigtail, and his coat-skirts, and the hair upon his head. The chain he drew was clasped about his middle. It was long, and

---

[77] John O'Neill, 'A Christmas Carol is not a secular tale', accessed 8/19. https://eu.detroitnews.com/story/opinion/2014/12/25/christmas-carol-secular/20887623/

wound about him like a tail; and it was made (for Scrooge observed it closely) of

cash-boxes, keys, padlocks, ledgers, deeds, and heavy purses wrought in steel.'[78]

The fact that this is a metaphorical chain is very clearly explained to us as readers.

' "You are fettered," said Scrooge, trembling. "Tell me why?"

"I wear the chain I forged in life," replied the Ghost. "I made it link by link, and yard

by yard; I girded it on of my own free will, and of my own free will I wore it. Is its

pattern strange to you?"

Scrooge trembled more and more.

"Or would you know," pursued the Ghost, "the weight and length of the strong coil

you bear yourself? It was full as heavy and as long as this, seven Christmas Eves

ago. You have laboured on it, since. It is a ponderous chain!" '[79]

Prisons, crimes and punishments are another big theme in all of Dickens' work. Spending time with his father in the Marshalsea debtors prison had shaped him, perhaps more than he'd realised at this point, and it makes a neat cameo in a later work, 'Little Dorrit'.

'Thirty years ago there stood, a few doors short of the church of Saint George, in the

borough of Southwark, on the left-hand side of the way going southward, the Mar-

shalsea Prison. It had stood there many years before, and it remained there some

years afterwards; but it is gone now, and the world is none the worse without it.

It was an oblong pile of barrack building, partitioned into squalid houses standing

---

[78] Dickens, *Christmas Books*, 16.

[79] Dickens, *Christmas Books*, 16.

back to back, so that there were no back rooms; environed by a narrow paved yard, hemmed in by high walls duly spiked at top. Itself a close and confined prison for debtors, it contained within it a much closer and more confined jail for smugglers. Offenders against the revenue laws, and defaulters to excise or customs who had incurred fines which they were unable to pay, were supposed to be incarcerated behind an iron-plated door closing up a second prison, consisting of a strong cell or two, and a blind alley some yard and a half wide, which formed the mysterious termination of the very limited skittle-ground in which the Marshalsea debtors bowled down their troubles.

Supposed to be incarcerated there, because the time had rather outgrown the strong cells and the blind alley. In practice they had come to be considered a little too bad, though in theory they were quite as good as ever; which may be observed to be the case at the present day with other cells that are not at all strong, and with other blind alleys that are stone-blind. Hence the smugglers habitually consorted with the debtors (who received them with open arms), except at certain constitutional moments when somebody came from some Office, to go through some form of overlooking something which neither he nor anybody else knew anything about. On these truly British occasions, the smugglers, if any, made a feint of walking into the strong cells and the blind alley, while this somebody pretended to do his something: and made a reality of walking out again as soon as he hadn't done it—neatly epitomising the administration of most of the public affairs in our right little, tight little, island.'[80]

Dickens' attitude to crime and punishment was not necessarily as simple as the above might make it seem, however.

[80] Charles Dickens, 'Little Dorrit', accessed 7/19. https://www.gutenberg.org/files/963/963-h/963-h.htm

'He approved of hard labour in prisons and felt satisfaction at witnessing a 'determined thief, swindler or vagrant, sweating profusely at the treadmill or the crank.' In Chapter 32 of Great Expectations, Pip momentarily sounds like a Daily Mail columnist when he makes ironic reference to a period where 'felons were not lodged and fed better than soldiers (to say nothing of paupers) and seldom set fire to their prisons with the excusable object of improving the flavour of their soup'. Once you had committed a criminal act, Dickens believed, you had to take responsibility for it, and incarceration was more about expiatory retribution and repentance than reform.

Yet Dickens also had a deep imaginative empathy with the criminal mind. In his earlier novels, he relished creating and inhabiting villains such as Quilp, Fagin, Bill Sikes and Uriah Heep, whose wickedness is caricatured and exploited for melodramatic effect, but he also understood how people were from childhood pushed or drawn into crime, in the face of heartless Poor Law institutions such as workhouses and appallingly inadequate housing, education, sanitation and moral guidance.'[81]

See how Marley is not himself redeemed, and is still condemned to suffer forever for his crime. He is only helping Scrooge to be kind, rather than it getting him out of his punishment. That said, Dickens' sympathy for prisoners is a common feature throughout all of his work, and Marley himself is quite appealing as it's clear he is in pain and full of regret. It was an American book tour that sparked Dickens' already strong feelings into a full campaign against the prison system he saw.

'Dickens went on to make the standard stops for a literary tourist of note in those times: factory towns, schools, hospitals, asylums—and prisons, including the notori-

---

[81] Rupert Christiansen, 'Dickens' Attitude to the Law', accessed 8/19. https://exec.typepad.com/greatexpectations/dickens-attitude-to-the-law.html

ous Eastern State Penitentiary in Philadelphia, where Dickens' reforming zeal was triggered.

Opened in 1829, Eastern was designed to implement the 19th-century American "Silent System"—day-in, day-out solitary confinement in cells 12 feet long by seven feet wide, lit by a small skylight 16 feet above the inmates' heads. Upon arrival, a prisoner was stripped, hooded, lectured by the warden and led to his cell, not to emerge again until his sentence was over. "He sees the prison-officers, but with that exception, he never looks upon a human countenance or hears a human voice," Dickens later wrote in American Notes. "He is a man buried alive; to be dug out in the slow round of years; and in the mean time dead to everything but torturing anxieties and horrible despair."

"As I walked among these solitary cells, and looked at the faces of the men within them, I tried to picture to myself the thoughts and feelings natural to their condition," Dickens reported. "I imagined the hood just taken off, and the scene of their captivity disclosed to them in all its dismal monotony. ... Every now and then there comes upon him a burning sense of the years that must be wasted in that stone coffin, and an agony so piercing in the recollection of those who are hidden from his view and knowledge, that he starts from his seat, and striding up and down the narrow room with both hands clasped on his uplifted head, hears spirits tempting him to beat his brains out on the wall."

Dickens, his novelist's sympathetic imagination at work, projected himself into the despairing mind of an Eastern prisoner, as he would later enter the souls of his great criminal characters, the murderers Anthony Chuzzlewit, Bradley Headstone, and John Jasper, and their guilty dreams and hallucinations.

The weary days pass on with solemn pace, like mourners at a funeral; and slowly he begins to feel that the whitewalls of the cell have something dreadful in them: that their colour is horrible: that their smooth surface chills his blood: that there is one hateful corner which torments him. Every morning when he wakes, he hides his head beneath the coverlet, and shudders to see the ghastly ceiling looking down upon him. The blessed light of day itself peeps in, an ugly phantom face, through the unchangeable crevice which is his prison window. By slow but sure degrees, the terrors of that hateful corner swell until they beset him at all times; invade his rest, make his dreams hideous, and his nights dreadful. At first, he took a strange dislike to it; feeling as though it gave birth in his brain to something of corresponding shape, which ought not to be there, and racked his head with pains. Then he began to fear it, then to dream of it, and of men whispering its name and pointing to it. Then he could not bear to look at it, nor yet to turn his back upon it. Now, it is every night the lurking-place of a ghost: a shadow:—a silent something, horrible to see, but whether bird, or beast, or muffled human shape, he cannot tell. ...A hideous figure, watching him till daybreak. ... If his period of confinement have been very long, the prospect of release bewilders and confuses him. His broken heart may flutter for a moment, when he thinks of the world outside, and what it might have been to him in all those lonely years, but that is all. The cell-door has been closed too long on all its hopes and cares.

Dickens tried to interview a sailor who had been imprisoned for 11 years and was about to be released. "'I am very glad to hear your time is nearly out.' What does he say? Nothing. Why does he stare at his hands, and pick the flesh upon his fingers, and raise his eyes for an instant ... to those bare walls which have seen his head turn grey? ... Does he never look men in the face, and does he always pluck at those hands

74

of his, as though he were bent on parting skin and bone?"

His conclusion:

A helpless, crushed and broken man. ...Better to have hanged him in the beginning than bring him to this pass, and send him forth to mingle with his kind, who are his kind no more. On the haggard face of every man among these prisoners, the same expression sat. I know not what to liken it to. It had something of that strained attention which we see upon the faces of the blind and deaf, mingled with a kind of horror, as though they had all been secretly terrified. In every little chamber that I entered, and at every grate through which I looked, I seemed to see the same appalling countenance. It lives in my memory, with the fascination of a remarkable picture. Parade before my eyes, a hundred men, with one among them newly released from this solitary suffering, and I would point him out.

Dickens urged his American readers to abolish the Silent System: "Nothing wholesome or good has ever had its growth in such unnatural solitude, [and] even a dog ... would pine and mope and rust away beneath its influence." But his common sense and common decency have not prevailed.'[82]

Alas, despite Dickens' loud voice, popular appeal and boundless energy, today's scholars feel he did not have that great an impact.

'"Although in his journalism and novels he attacked specific targets - Poor Law legislation in Oliver Twist, the brutal Yorkshire schools in Nicholas Nickleby, the law

---

[82] Michael Stern, 'Like Being Buried Alive: Charles Dickens on Solitary Confinement in American Prisons', accessed 8/19. https://prospect.org/article/being-%e2%80%9cburied-alive%e2%80%9d-charles-dickens-solitary-confinement-america%e2%80%99s-prisons

[Pickwick Papers and Bleak House], government bureaucracy, lethargy and nepotism in Little Dorrit, extremist utilitarianism in Hard Times - it's hard to trace any direct consequences on reformist legislation in any of those areas to Dickens's influence," argues *Prof Malcolm Andrews, editor of the Dickensian, journal of the Dickens Fellowship.'*[83]

Dickens will always be remembered as someone who did try hard to make the system of punishment fairer and more humane, despite this lack of impact.

[83] Matthew Davis, 'Did Charles Dickens really save poor children and clean up the slums?', accessed 8/19. https://www.bbc.co.uk/news/magazine-16907648

Fred and Family

Before we discuss the jolly Fred, we need to think about who he is demographically. Fred, and his uncle Ebeneezer, are energetic members of the newly emerged middle class, and the same sort of people who would buy Dickens' books. What does that mean, exactly?

'The Victorian middle-class is largely associated with the growth of cities and the expansion of the economy. The term was used from around the mid-eighteenth century to describe those people below the aristocracy but above the workers. As a social category, the 'middling sort' always referred to a broad band of the population, but this diversity increased in the nineteenth century. Alongside the businessmen associated with the growth of manufacturing, the period saw the increased numbers of small entrepreneurs. Shopkeepers and merchants who undertook to transport and retail the fruits of industry and empire. The increased scale of industry and oversees trade, together with the expansion of empire fuelled the proliferation of commerce and finance such as banks, insurance companies, shipping and railways. This system needed administrating by clerks, managers and salaried professionals. The expansion of cities, towns and the economy produced new spaces that needing regulating and running. The Victorian period witnessed the massive expansion of local government and the centralised state, providing occupations for a vast strata of civil servants, teachers, doctors, lawyers and government officials as well as the clerks and assistants which helped these institutions and services to operate.

Such diversity makes a satisfactory definition of the middle-class impossible. There is no clear relationship to the means of production. Although there were some individuals that accumulated spectacular wealth in the nineteenth century through entrepreneurial activity, there were many more businessmen who scraped a living and

77

many who worked for wages as public servants, managers or clerks. The economic boundary of the 'middle-class' was not clear. Some members of the middle-class used their wealth to buy land and stately homes, becoming as rich, if not richer than the aristocracy. At the same time, many members of the skilled working class could earn as much if not more than some members of the lower middle-class.'[84]

Fred and Scrooge live in a society in transition. This new group were increasing in size and power, but couldn't rely on the moral codes that had guided the ruling classes in the past. They had to find their own way, as Dickens did. Scrooge, just like Dickens had seen his fortunes rise and fall as part of this class, and fictional Fred was the beneficiary of their efforts. The real Fred, however, was nowhere near as secure.

'There is no question among scholars that Fred was probably based on Frederick Dickens, Charles' favourite brother of his youth. Fred had been born on July 4, 1820. Fred attended a schooling Hampstead with their brother Alfred Dickens for two years, until their father join Dickens could no longer afford the fees. At the end of the school day, the boys would be collected by their older brother, Charles.'[85]

For much of the brothers' lives they got on very well with each other, and Fred even cared for Charles' children when he away on a tour of America. However, their relationship began to sour over money by 1843.

---

[84] Donna Loftus, 'The Rise of the Victorian Middle Class', accessed 8/19. https://www.bbc.co.uk/history/british/victorians/middle_classes_01.shtml

[85] Devito, *Inventing Scrooge*, 63.

'Fred, although his . . .salary had been increased, was falling into his father's extravagant ways. A creditor at Gray's Inn sent Dickens [Fred's bill and] Fred seemed to resent the way that Dickens had resolved the matter'[86]

Scrooge's line upon Fred's first appearance now seems like it could come straight from the mouth of a frustrated older brother such as Charles:

'What's Christmas time to you but a time for paying bills without money; a time for finding yourself a year older, but not an hour richer; a time for balancing your books and having every item in 'em through a round dozen of months presented dead against you?'[87]

Fred, who had previously been a jolly visitor to the Dickens family home, was notably absent, especially at Christmas. Perhaps then, it's Fred's reply which comes straight from Dickens' mouth:

"There are many things from which I might have derived good, by which I have not profited, I dare say," returned the nephew. "Christmas among the rest. But I am sure I have always thought of Christmas time, when it has come round—apart from the veneration due to its sacred name and origin, if anything belonging to it can be apart from that—as a good time; a kind, forgiving, charitable, pleasant time; the only time I know of, in the long calendar of the year, when men and women seem by one consent to open their shut-up hearts freely, and to think of people below them as if they really were fellow-passengers to the grave, and not another race of creatures bound on other journeys. And therefore, uncle, though it has never put a scrap of gold or silver in

---

[86] Devito, *Inventing Scrooge*, 67.

[87] Dickens, *Christmas Books*, 19.

my pocket, I believe that it has done me good, and will do me good; and I say, God bless it!"[88]

---

[88] Dickens, *Christmas Books*, 19.

The Ghost of Christmas Past and Childhood

Dickens' childhood was somewhat grim from the age of twelve onwards. Charles, who had grown up as a relatively normal young man, had found himself sent out to work to support his family by working in a blacking factory. He later related his experiences to his best friend, John Forster:

"It is wonderful to me how I could have been so easily cast away at such an age. It is wonderful to me that, even after my descent into the poor little drudge I had been since we came to London, no one had compassion enough on me — a child of singular abilities, quick, eager, delicate, and soon hurt, bodily or mentally — to suggest that something might have been spared, as certainly it might have been, to place me at any common school. Our friends, I take it, were tired out. No one made any sign. My father and mother were quite satisfied. They could hardly have been more so if I had been twenty years of age, distinguished at a grammar-school, and going to Cambridge.

"The blacking-warehouse was the last house on the left-hand side of the way, at old Hungerford Stairs. It was a crazy, tumble-down old house, abutting of course on the river, and literally overrun with rats. Its wainscoted rooms, and its rotten floors and staircase, and the old gray rats swarming down in the cellars, and the sound of their squeaking and scuffling coming up the stairs at all times, and the dirt and decay of the place, rise up visibly before me, as if I were there again. The counting-house was on the first floor, looking over the coal-barges and the river. There was a recess in it, in which I was to sit and work. My work was to cover the pots of paste-blacking; first with a piece of oil-paper, and then with a piece of blue paper; to tie them round with a string; and then to clip the paper close and neat, all round, until it looked as smart as a pot of ointment from an apothecary's shop. When a certain number of grosses of

pots had attained this pitch of perfection, I was to paste on each a printed label, and then go on again with more pots. Two or three other boys were kept at similar duty down-stairs on similar wages. One of them came up, in a ragged apron and a paper cap, on the first Monday morning, to show me the trick of using the string and tying the knot. His name was Bob Fagin; and I took the liberty of using his name, long afterwards, in Oliver Twist.

No words can express the secret agony of my soul as I sunk into this companionship; compared these every-day associates with those of my happier childhood; and felt my early hopes of growing up to be a learned and distinguished man, crushed in my breast. The deep remembrance of the sense I had of being utterly neglected and hopeless; of the shame I felt in my position; of the misery it was to my young heart to believe that, day by day, what I had learned, and thought, and delighted in, and raised my fancy and my emulation up by, was passing away from me, never to be brought back any more; cannot be written. My whole nature was so penetrated with the grief and humiliation of such considerations, that even now, famous and caressed and happy, I often forget in my dreams that I have a dear wife and children; even that I am a man; and wander desolately back to that time of my life.'[89]

Poor Charles believed this was one of the formative experiences of his young life. He never spoke about this to anyone until many years later, after a harrowing bout of interviews for a charity project, when he mentioned it in passing to Forster. This is now one of the legends that make up the story of Dickens' life.

Why use the image of a child across so many of his books? To answer this, we have to step slightly further back in time, to the eighteenth century.

[89] Forster, John (2019 ed), *The Life of Charles Dickens*, UK: Forgotten Books, 25.

'In the early modern period and undoubtedly associated with the emergence of 'individualism' and the rise of the middle class and the 'domestic', there emerged an idea of the child quite unlike earlier conceptions, which had assumed children to be essentially animalistic and uninteresting, or merely deficient, undeveloped and incomplete adults'[90]

Enter into this scene the Romantic poets William Wordsworth and William Blake, who argued that children represented a natural state closer to how God intended all humans to be. Dickens' experiences as a boy, he felt, were incredibly important to the man he grew up to be.

'Pity for his own lost childhood undoubtedly made him especially receptive to the Wordsworthian conception of childhood and this sensitivity...[led to] not just a reverence for the child but an often intense fear for the child's welfare and a sometimes morbid sentimentality...'[91]

Assuming that Dickens did follow Wordsworth's philosophy that our childhood experiences shape who we are, then it's absolutely key that we get a glimpse into Scrooge's childhood to get a picture of where his unpleasantness originated from.

Could we see some of Dickens' child characters based on his own clan of ten children? Not really. As Emily Witt notes:

'Dickens was 25 when his eldest son Charley was born. The author already enjoyed massive popular success, with The Pickwick Papers in serialization and Oliver Twist

---

[90] Jordan, *The Cambridge Companion*, 92.

[91] Jordan, *The Cambridge Companion*, 93.

in the works. While it's certain that having so many toddlers underfoot likely affected, say, Dickens's description of the Jellyby household in Bleak House ("We passed several more children on the way up, whom it was difficult to avoid treading on in the dark ..."), it would be hard to identify any parallels between the extraordinary juveniles in Dickens's books and his own brood.'[92]

Similarly, given the compassion and tenderness with which he approaches the character of Tiny Tim, it would be reasonable to think Dickens was a loving and kind father. He definitely was while the children were young, but eventually he became incredibly critical of his offspring.

'Having earned his success and overcome childhood poverty while still a teenager through his own impressive energy and drive, his children's complacency and lack of ambition disconcerted him. "I think he has less fixed purpose and energy than I could have supposed possible in my son," writes Dickens of Charley. (This "lassitude of character" is attributed to Charley's mother.) Of Frank: "A good steady fellow ... but not at all brilliant." And Plorn[93]: "he seems to have been born without a groove. It cannot be helped. He is not aspiring or imaginative in his own behalf." '[94]

Despite his despair towards his own children, Dickens became a supporter of education for all, as it:

'had the potential to rescue working-class children from the ravages of industrialisation and from the dangers that lurked in the sprawling city.'[95]

---

[92] Emily Witt, 'Daddy Issues: On the Worthless Brood of Charles Dickens', accessed 8/19. https://observer.com/2012/12/daddy-issues-on-the-worthless-brood-of-charles-dickens/

[93] His nickname for his son Edward.

[94] Witt, 'Daddy Issues'.

[95] Unknown, 'Dickens and the Victorian City', accessed 8/19. http://dickens.port.ac.uk/education/

Ragged Schools interested him in particular. These were institutions set up by independent and charitably minded benefactors to teach the poorest children the basics of literacy, maths and Christian doctrine. There was no external financial support for these outside the kindly individuals, and these philanthropists provided invaluable help for the children who needed it most.

As a compulsive letter writer, we know exactly what Dickens thought of the provision for education, which he saw as he visited a specific Ragged School in Portsmouth:

"On Thursday night, I went to the Ragged School; and an awful sight it is. I blush to quote Oliver Twist for an authority. . . The school is held in three most wretched rooms on the first floor of a rotten house: every plank, and timber, and brick, and lath, and piece of plaster in which, shakes as you walk. One room is devoted to the girls: two to the boys. The former are much the better-looking — I cannot say better dressed, for there is no such thing as dress among the seventy pupils; certainly not the elements of a whole suit of clothes, among them all. I have very seldom seen, in all the strange and dreadful things I have seen in London and elsewhere anything so shocking as the dire neglect of soul and body exhibited in these children. And although I know; and am as sure as it is possible for one to be of anything which has not happened; that in the prodigious misery and ignorance of the swarming masses of mankind in England, the seeds of its certain ruin are sown, I never saw that Truth so staring out in hopeless characters, as it does from the walls of this place. The children in the Jails are almost as common sights to me as my own; but these are worse,

for they have not arrived there yet, but are as plainly and certainly travelling there,

as they are to their Graves..." [96]

This school described above was indeed grim, as a former pupil verified:

'*...dark, dingy, cold and miserable most of the time...I never saw a fire, there was no*

gas. Light and heat cost money, and had to be done without. Besides,

these luxuries would tend to make the boys effeminate and the object then was, to

turn out hardy boys...'[97]

Dickens fought back against the conditions that these children faced in their lives in the best way he could: namely, by criticising those who did not support children in his books, especially in 'Hard Times'. When we see the pitiful faces of Ignorance and Want, and poor Tiny Tim struggling with his crutch, we see this agenda given human features.

It wasn't merely schools that Dickens wanted to fight for. It was also for children's freedom against having to work in horrific conditions, and critics believe this may have been what started the whole Christmas Carol project in the first place.

'*Dickens first conceived of his project as a pamphlet, which he planned on calling,*

"An Appeal to the People of England on behalf of the Poor Man's Child." But in less

than a week of thinking about it, he decided instead to embody his arguments in a

story, with a main character of pitiable depth. So what might have been a polemic to

harangue, instead became a story for which audiences hungered.

---

[96] Reproduced in Ian Dooley, 'Charles Dickens Describes a Ragged School to Angela Burdett-Coutts', accessed 8/19. https://blogs.princeton.edu/cotsen/2016/06/the-ragged-school-a-letter-from-charles-dickens-to-angela-burdett-coutts/

[97] 'Dickens and the Victorian City'.

Dickens set out to write his pamphlet-turned-book in spring 1843, having just read government report on child labor in the United Kingdom. The report took the form of a compilation of interviews with children—compiled by a journalist friend of Dickens—that detailed their crushing labors.

Dickens read the testimony of girls who sewed dresses for the expanding market of middle class consumers; they regularly worked 16 hours a day, six days a week, rooming—like Martha Cratchit—above the factory floor. He read of 8-year-old children who dragged coal carts through tiny subterranean passages over a standard 11-hour workday. These were not exceptional stories, but ordinary. Dickens wrote to one of the government investigators that the descriptions left him "stricken."

This new, brutal reality of child labor was the result of revolutionary changes in British society. The population of England had grown 64% between Dickens' birth in 1812 and the year of the child labor report. Workers were leaving the countryside to crowd into new manufacturing centers and cities. Meanwhile, there was a revolution in the way goods were manufactured: cottage industry was upended by a trend towards workers serving as unskilled cogs laboring in the pre-cursor of the assembly line, hammering the same nail or gluing the same piece—as an 11-year-old Dickens had to do—hour after hour, day after day.

More and more, employers thought of their workers as tools as interchangeable as any nail or gluepot. Workers were becoming like commodities: not individual humans, but mere resources, their value measured to the ha-penny by how many nails they could hammer in an hour. But in a time of dearth—the 1840s earned the nickname "The Hungry '40s"—the poor took what work they could arrange. And who worked for the lowest wages? Children.'[98]

Tempting as it might be to link Dickens to Marx or other thinkers who wanted profound social change, this is not what Dickens thought was needed to help these child labourers.

'What he wrote was that employers are responsible for the well-being of their employees. Their workers are not of value only to the extent to which they contribute to a product for the cheapest possible labor cost. They are of value as "fellow-passengers to the grave," in the words of Scrooge's nephew, "and not another race of creatures bound on other journeys." Employers owe their employees as human beings — no better, but no worse, than themselves.'[99]

As with everything else in A Christmas Carol, it all comes down to social responsibility for everyone, young and old, rich and poor.

---

[98] John Broich, 'The real reason Dickens wrote A Christmas Carol', accessed 8/19. https://time.com/4597964/history-charles-dickens-christmas-carol/

[99] Broich, 'The real reason'.

The Ghost of Christmas Present and Dickens' London

The London that Dickens presents us in A Christmas Carol is a magical and contradictory place. Take the description in Stave Three, for example:

'*Holly, mistletoe, red berries, ivy, turkeys, geese, game, poultry, brawn, meat, pigs, sausages, oysters, pies, puddings, fruit, and punch, all vanished instantly. So did the room, the fire, the ruddy glow, the hour of night, and they stood in the city streets on Christmas morning, where (for the weather was severe) the people made a rough, but brisk and not unpleasant kind of music, in scraping the snow from the pavement in front of their dwellings, and from the tops of their houses, whence it was mad delight to the boys to see it come plumping down into the road below, and splitting into artificial little snow-storms.*

The house fronts looked black enough, and the windows blacker, contrasting with the smooth white sheet of snow upon the roofs, and with the dirtier snow upon the ground; which last deposit had been ploughed up in deep furrows by the heavy wheels of carts and waggons; furrows that crossed and re-crossed each other hundreds of times where the great streets branched off; and made intricate channels, hard to trace in the thick yellow mud and icy water. The sky was gloomy, and the shortest streets were choked up with a dingy mist, half thawed, half frozen, whose heavier particles descended in a shower of sooty atoms, as if all the chimneys in Great Britain had, by one consent, caught fire, and were blazing away to their dear hearts' content. There was nothing very cheerful in the climate or the town, and yet was there an air of cheerfulness abroad that the clearest summer air and brightest summer sun might have endeavoured to diffuse in vain.'[100]

---

[100] Dickens, *Christmas Books*, 42.

The contrasts of dark and light, happiness and fear, and hope and hopeless-
ness are partly what attracted Dickens to London. While he was born in
Portsmouth, he lived in London from perhaps the age of eleven onwards, and
found it a huge source of inspiration. He was also one of the first writers in
decades to use London widely in his fiction. Perhaps this was a marketing
decision as many of his readers would have been part of the growing population of the capital, but it was also a place that represented his own ideas
about how society could change, since:

*'During Dickens' lifetime, London was more excavated, more cut about, more rebuilt
and more extended than at any time in its previous history.'*[101]

He was someone who wished for social change, and he could see this every
time he walked around London.

*'His modern vision articulates the city scene as a site of dialectic contradictions. For
Dickens, London was not only a conflicted city, in transition, but one whose explosive
urban vitality depends on the yoking together of its contradictions.'*[102]

Dickens engaged with the city through personal experience. His early newspaper columns, published as 'Sketches by Boz', focused on street life as he
saw it on his walks around the capital. He was a lifelong observer of the
people around him and, as we have already seen, was not afraid to use them
as inspiration for his fictional work.

---

[101] Jordan, *The Cambridge Companion*, 106.

[102] Jordan, *The Cambridge Companion*, 112.

This observation brings us on to the idea of being a spectator: Scrooge watches others during the Ghost of Christmas Present's visit, yet he can't be seen himself.

'Scrooge is presented not with real life but with images of real life, and the reader is presented with images of images of real life. The reader is positioned as a spectator of a Scrooge who is, in turn, a spectator of the images which are presented to him by his ghostly visitants, and those images always focus on the denial and/ or enjoyment of the pleasures of consumption.'[103]

So, in a sense, the Ghost of Christmas Present puts us in the same position as Scrooge himself, watching events that we can't influence. At that point, seeing the Cratchits' and Fred's Christmases, Dickens has made us empathise with Scrooge by putting us in his shoes, as well as making us empathise with him as he observes people walking around town.

From a modern perspective, the idea of constantly watching others and being watched ourselves can seem creepy. The critic D.A. Miller addressed this explicitly in 1988, saying:

'[Dickens and other similar writers] systematically participate in a general economy of policing power'[104]

In other words, Dickens invites us (the average reader) to judge Scrooge and condemn him for his bad behaviour, even though objectively we know there is no 'correct' way to celebrate Christmas. His party plans aren't the real issue, however. His morality very much is.

---

[103] Pykett, *Critical Issues*, 93.

[104] Quoted in Pykett, *Critical Issues*, 18.

'Dickens believed in the ethical and political potential of literature, and the novel in particular, and he treated his fiction as a springboard for debates about moral and social reform. In his novels of social analysis Dickens became an outspoken critic of unjust economic and social conditions. His deeply-felt social commentaries helped raise the collective awareness of the reading public.' [105]

By judging Scrooge, we are judging ourselves and hopefully realising that we need to do more to help others.

---

[105] Dr Andrzej Diniejko, 'Charles Dickens as Social Commentator and Critic', accessed 7/19.
http://www.victorianweb.org/authors/dickens/diniejko.html

The Ghost of Christmas Future and Death

Death, sadly, comes to us all, but Scrooge's encounter with death is far more personal than most are likely to experience.

'There is no question that the Ghost of Christmas Yet to Come is a loosely dressed version of the Angel of Death, a popular character in Western literature. The concept of death as a sentient entity has existed in many societies since the beginning of history. Certainly characters like the Grim Reaper, for example, date back to the fifteenth century. The most popular version was shown as a skeletal figure carrying a large scythe and clothes with a black cloak with a hood.'[106]

The peculiar Victorian obsession with death is well documented, so it can be argued that what truly scares Scrooge in Stave Four is not that he will die, but that he will not be granted the 'good death' that a middle class Victorian would hope for.

A good death is one that is moving, sentimental and inspiring. Take another Dickensian death, that of Little Nell in 'The Old Curiosity Shop', for example:

'Waving them off with his hand, and calling softly to her as he went, he stole into the room. They who were left behind, drew close together, and after a few whispered words—not unbroken by emotion, or easily uttered—followed him. They moved so gently, that their footsteps made no noise; but there were sobs from among the group, and sounds of grief and mourning.

For she was dead. There, upon her little bed, she lay at rest. The solemn stillness was

---

[106] Devito, *Inventing Scrooge,* 162.

no marvel now.

She was dead. No sleep so beautiful and calm, so free from trace of pain, so fair to look upon. She seemed a creature fresh from the hand of God, and waiting for the breath of life; not one who had lived and suffered death.

Her couch was dressed with here and there some winter berries and green leaves, gathered in a spot she had been used to favour. 'When I die, put near me something that has loved the light, and had the sky above it always.' Those were her words.

She was dead. Dear, gentle, patient, noble Nell was dead. Her little bird—a poor slight thing the pressure of a finger would have crushed—was stirring nimbly in its cage; and the strong heart of its child mistress was mute and motionless for ever.

Where were the traces of her early cares, her sufferings, and fatigues? All gone. Sorrow was dead indeed in her, but peace and perfect happiness were born; imaged in her tranquil beauty and profound repose.

And still her former self lay there, unaltered in this change. Yes. The old fireside had smiled upon that same sweet face; it had passed, like a dream, through haunts of misery and care; at the door of the poor schoolmaster on the summer evening, before the furnace fire upon the cold wet night, at the still bedside of the dying boy, there had been the same mild lovely look. So shall we know the angels in their majesty, after death.'[107]

---

[107] Charles Dickens, 'The Old Curiosity Shop', accessed 7/19. https://www.gutenberg.org/files/700/700-h/700-h.htm

THE FUNERAL OF CHARLES DICKENS

It will be a gratifying surprise to the admirers of Charles Dickens to learn that his remains have been entombed in Westminster Abbey. Yesterday morning, Dickens was privately buried in "Poets' Corner." Through the influence of Dean Stanley, and owing to the universal wish that he should be laid to rest with the other worthies of English literature, the family consented to depart from the oft-expressed desire of the deceased to be buried near Rochester, and allow his remains to be removed to London. They, however, determined that the proceedings should be conducted as privately as possible, and when the body arrived at the Charing Cross Railway Station, at nine o'clock yesterday morning, no one was there to receive it but the friends who had been invited to take part in the ceremony. Mr. Dickens's well-known repugnance to ostentatious display was well known, and his wishes were faithfully observed. There were no trappings about the hearse or the three mourning coaches, and none of the mourners wore any but the plainest emblems of mourning. Even hatbands were dispensed with. The following relatives and friends occupied the coaches:— Mr. C. Dickens, jun. Mr. Harry Dickens, Miss Dickens, Mrs. C. Dickens, jun. Mrs. Austin (Mr. Dickens's sister), Miss G. Hogarth, Mr. John Forster, Mr. C. Collins, Mr. F. Beard, Mr. Ouvry, Mr. Wilkie Collins, and Mr. Edmund Dickens. The *cortège* proceeded along the Strand, down Charing Cross, Whitehall, and King-street to the Abbey door, where Dean Stanley and the clergy of the Abbey were in waiting. The service was read by the Dean. Beyond a voluntary played on the organ, there was no musical accompaniment. The coffin was of mahogany, and upon it were placed exotic ferns, a chaplet of camelias, and red and white roses. On the plate was the simple inscription: "Charles Dickens. Born 7th Feb. 1812. Died 9th June 1870." So recent was the determination of Mr. Dickens's family to permit the funeral to take place in the Abbey that it was not till midnight on Monday that the grave was prepared, when in fact a grave had already been dug in Rochester Cathedral. At Dickens's feet lie Sheridan and Samuel Johnson, and in their immediate vicinity are the coffins of Southey, Campbell, and Gray. Dickens's immediate neighbours to the right are Richard Cumberland, the essayist and dramatist, and Handel. To the left of Dickens are the coffins of Macaulay, Addison, and other eminent writers. A bust of Thackeray is placed on the wall above, and on the opposite side of the transept is the monument of Shakspere.

The grave was kept open during the day, and when the circumstance became known thousands of visitors flocked to see it—members of Parliament, co-workers of Dickens in the field of letters, working men, and people of all classes, who desired to take a last look at the resting-place of one who had contributed so much to their enjoyment.

The perfect death has been granted to the little girl: non-violent, beautiful and designed to tug at the heartstrings.

Of course, Dickens had no idea that when he died, he would have the ultimate 'good death'.[108]

Funerals, as shown above by the report on the previous page, were seriously important to your average Victorian. How, exactly, were you supposed to show your feelings for your loved ones if you didn't go all out for their memorial service? It was a huge industry and to participate in it fully, you were expected to spend a lot of money and follow a bizarrely complex set of rules.

'Following Victoria's example, it became customary for families to go through elaborate rituals to commemorate their dead. This included wearing mourning clothes, having a lavish (and expensive) funeral, curtailing social behavior for a set period of time, and erecting an ornate monument on the grave[109].

Mourning clothes were a family's outward display of their inner feelings. The rules for who wore what and for how long were complicated, and were outlined in popular journals or household manuals such as The Queen and Cassell's – both very popular among Victorian housewives. They gave copious instructions about appropriate mourning etiquette. If your second cousin died and you wanted to know what sort of mourning clothes you should wear and for how long, you consulted The Queen or Cassell's or other manuals.

For deepest mourning clothes were to be black, symbolic of spiritual darkness. Dresses for deepest mourning were usually made of non-reflective paramatta silk or the cheaper bombazine – many of the widows in Dickens' novels wore bombazine.

---

[108] Margaret Holborn, 'Charles Dickens dies - archive, June 1870', accessed 8/19. https://uploads.guim.co.uk/2017/06/07/Manchester_Guardian_15_June_1870_report_of_funeral_of_Charles_Dickens.pdf

[109] If this interests you, I hugely recommend the tour of Highgate Cemetery.

Dresses were trimmed with crape, a hard, scratchy silk with a peculiar crimped appearance produced by heat. Crape is particularly associated with mourning because it doesn't combine well with any other clothing – you can't wear velvet or satin or lace or embroidery with it. After a specified period the crape could be removed – this was called "slighting the mourning." The color of cloth lightened as mourning went on, to grey, mauve, and white – called half-mourning. Jewelry was limited to jet, a hard, black coal-like material sometimes combined with woven hair of the deceased.

Men had it easy – they simply wore their usual dark suits along with black gloves, hatbands and cravats. Children were not expected to wear mourning clothes, though girls sometimes wore white dresses.

The length of mourning depended on your relationship to the deceased. The different periods of mourning dictated by society were expected to reflect your natural period of grief. Widows were expected to wear full mourning for two years. Everyone else presumably suffered less – for children mourning parents or vice versa the period of time was one year, for grandparents and siblings six months, for aunts and uncles two months, for great uncles and aunts six weeks, for first cousins four weeks.

Someone had to provide the clothes quickly to mourners. Many shops catered to the trade; the largest and best known of them in London was Jay's of Regent Street. Opened in 1841 as a kind of warehouse for mourners, Jay's provided every conceivable item of clothing you and your family could need. And you were bound to be repeat customers: it was considered bad luck to keep mourning clothes – particularly crape – in the house after mourning ended. That meant buying clothes all over again when the next loved one passed. Mourning was a lucrative business.'[110]

Scrooge's meagre funeral, with no attendants, hit both the Victorian readership and Scrooge with the reality of how bad Scrooge's life really had been.

'There is an unending list of rules and regulations regarding death, burials, and mourning in this era. Not to follow the rules meant that the offender was somehow immoral or dishonouring the deceased.'[111]

He finished his life as a morally disgusting and dishonourable man. This was how society had judged him, as seen by his small tombstone. What could be more awful to any Victorian man than being seen as a terrible person for all eternity? Moreover, it marked him as a failure. Scrooge must have been in business for a long time, and yet he's shown that it has all come to nothing when the Ghost of Christmas Yet To Come reveals his tombstone.

'For the same reasons that the well-appointed funerals of the wealthy and prominent came to signify their pre-eminent position in society, the ignominious funerals of the poor came to signify the opposite-their absolute exclusion from the social body. Social standing came increasingly to depend on acquired rather than on inherited attributes, on earned wealth, on membership in a variety of voluntaristic organizations, on one's philanthropic or entrepreneurial prominence. In a world of this sort, where public standing had become intimately linked with the importance one had earned in the eyes of one's fellow men, no man's reputation could be finally assured until the

[110] Tracy Chevalier, 'Victorian Morning Etiquette', accessed 7/19. https://www.tchevalier.com/fallingangels/bckgrnd/mourning/

[111] Marilyn A Mendoza, 'Death and Mourning Practices in the Victorian Age', accessed 7/19. https://www.psychologytoday.com/gb/blog/understanding-grief/201812/death-and-mourning-practices-in-the-victorian-age

moment of his death. Funerals thus became the ritual occasions for definitively mark-

ing social place, and the imaginative vehicle for contemplating one's ultimate fate in

the public eye. For the rich and successful, for those with social ties, the funeral

could be anticipated with equanimity. Not so for the poor and friendless; it haunted

them as the specter of failure. '112

Just like Dickens, he has transcended class, but not in a good way. Despite his riches he will be seen as a shameful pauper for the rest of time. He's even lost his curtains. Much like his status as a batchelor without a loving home life, this lack of a lavish funeral also marks him forever as an outsider, excluded by the rest of society.

'The funerals of more ordinary men, like the funerals of the great, were essentially

rituals of inclusion; in contrast, however, they expressed the deceased's place in the

local community rather than in the social order generally. There was no outside

world, as was represented in heraldic funerals by those who watched it-its audience-

against which the rank of the deceased was measured. The participants in the ordi-

nary funeral were also its audience; there was no other public for whose edification

the ritual was being performed. In contrast to heraldic funerals, the funerals of ordi-

nary men followed no set forms. Status, and not wealth alone, marked one's place in

the local community'113

As Dickens himself wrote shortly after finding the tombstone of Ebeneezer Scroggie:

---

[112] Thomas Laquer, 'Bodies Death and Pauper Funerals', accessed 7/19. https://pdfs.semantic-scholar.org/a0f3/be5d5aae6e4cc07add3cf7a96b570533170a.pdf

[113] Lacquer, 'Bodies...'

'To be remembered through eternity for only being mean seemed the greatest testament to a life wasted.'[114]

Death does not only feature in Stave Four, however. Death occurs from the very start of the novel, which the many, many mentions of Marley's death.

'Marley was dead: to begin with. There is no doubt whatever about that. The register of his burial was signed by the clergyman, the clerk, the undertaker, and the chief mourner. Scrooge signed it: and Scrooge's name was good upon 'Change, for anything he chose to put his hand to. Old Marley was as dead as a door-nail.

Mind! I don't mean to say that I know, of my own knowledge, what there is particularly dead about a door-nail. I might have been inclined, myself, to regard a coffin-nail as the deadest piece of ironmongery in the trade. But the wisdom of our ancestors is in the simile; and my unhallowed hands shall not disturb it, or the Country's done for. You will therefore permit me to repeat, emphatically, that Marley was as dead as a door-nail.

Scrooge knew he was dead? Of course he did. How could it be otherwise? Scrooge and he were partners for I don't know how many years. Scrooge was his sole executor, his sole administrator, his sole assign, his sole residuary legatee, his sole friend, and sole mourner. And even Scrooge was not so dreadfully cut up by the sad event, but that he was an excellent man of business on the very day of the funeral, and solemnised it with an undoubted bargain.

The mention of Marley's funeral brings me back to the point I started from. There is no doubt that Marley was dead. This must be distinctly understood, or nothing won-

---

[114] Devito, Inventing Scrooge, 45.

derful can come of the story I am going to relate. If we were not perfectly convinced that Hamlet's Father died before the play began, there would be nothing more remarkable in his taking a stroll at night, in an easterly wind, upon his own ramparts, than there would be in any other middle-aged gentleman rashly turning out after dark in a breezy spot—say Saint Paul's Churchyard for instance—literally to astonish his son's weak mind.'[115]

Why bring death into such a cheerful season? Michael Faber finds this question exhilarating:

'Dickens leaves Jesus alone and concentrates on what excites his imagination most: death, grotesquery, poverty, indignity, death, clownish pranks, death, dancing and food. Oh, and did I mention death?

The novella's famous first line, "Marley was dead, to begin with", establishes many things at once. It avoids the grandiloquent rhetoric many people might expect of the opening paragraph of a Victorian novel, in favour of a terse, muscular address. It allows Dickens to indulge his love of topsy-turvyness, insisting that what sounds like a story's end is in fact the beginning. It delivers a gentle shock to those readers who might have expected a Christmas story to begin in a festive spirit. It promises supernatural fun, because it comes straight after the chapter title "Marley's Ghost", a tip-off that Marley can't be quite as dead as the narrator claims. And, although Ebenezer Scrooge has not yet spoken, it chimes in with what we'll soon recognise as the miser's characteristic tone: over-emphatic insistence that he's right about everything, when we know that he's lamentably mistaken. So, in that one line - six short words! - Dickens encapsulates the philosophical tension of the entire story: the tension between

---

[115] Dickens, *Christmas Books*, 1.

101

blinkered certitude and open-eyed humility.

Most of all, though, the opening line allows Dickens to put death prominently on the menu. Despite his status - in his own time, and in ours - as the ultimate family entertainer, Dickens was energised by all things grim and gruesome. Foulness got his creative juices flowing. A Christmas Carol is an unevenly written work, creaky in places, and showing signs of haste, but there's no mistaking Dickens's full engagement when he accompanies Scrooge into a filthy slum crowded with garbage and offal, where dark secrets are "bred and hidden in mountains of unseemly rags, masses of corrupted fat, and sepulchres of bones". Note, too, the macabre hilarity of the moment when Marley's ghost takes off the bandage wrapped round his head "as if it were too warm to wear indoors" and his whole lower jaw drops down on to his chest (a horror-movie "special effect" that wouldn't be out of place in Sam Raimi's Evil Dead films.) Also, while Dickens is doubtless sincere in his disapproval of Scrooge's misanthropy, we can sense his wicked glee at Scrooge's declaration that "every idiot who goes about with 'Merry Christmas' on his lips should be boiled with his own pudding, and buried with a stake of holly through his heart".[116]

The black humour relating to death is partly what makes A Christmas Carol so entertaining, and takes the edge off the saccharine sweetness.

[116] Michael Faber, 'Spectral Pleasures', accessed 8/19. https://www.theguardian.com/books/2005/dec/24/featuresreviews.guardianreview22

Redemption

Scrooge is, of course, redeemed by the end of the novel.

'Scrooge was better than his word. He did it all, and infinitely more; and to Tiny Tim, who did not die, he was a second father. He became as good a friend, as good a master, and as good a man, as the good old city knew, or any other good old city, town, or borough, in the good old world. Some people laughed to see the alteration in him, but he let them laugh, and little heeded them; for he was wise enough to know that nothing ever happened on this globe, for good, at which some people did not have their fill of laughter in the outset; and knowing that such as these would be blind anyway, he thought it quite as well that they should wrinkle up their eyes in grins, as have the malady in less attractive forms. His own heart laughed: and that was quite enough for him.'[117]

Dickens loved a happy ending, and through the power of love and Christmas, Scrooge has made it. But what caused this redemption within the old miser?

'The final crystallization of his character solidified when his fiancée released him from his vow to marry. She said, "Another idol has displaced me... A golden one. You are changed. When your vow was made, you were another man... I release you. With a full heart, for the love of him you once were." She had realized the old Ebenezer was gone. His character jelled into one that she no longer recognized nor loved. It was too late. Scrooge would play out his character story of hardness, cruelty, and the inability to love.

Indeed, with the ghost of Christmas Past, Scrooge visited his ex-fiancée and her fami-

---

[117] Dickens, *Christmas Books*, 75.

ly. He realized that he missed out on love, and being a father with a happy home. He saw that he would die like Marley, all alone. He saw her daughter and "He thought that such another creature, quite as graceful and as full of promise, might have called him father." This brought out such regret and pain.

Scrooge was deeply affected by the past. He wept and mourned his pain. He began to feel genuine regret for his life decisions. He regretted hardening his heart to love. He regretted how he conducted himself with a meanness of spirit. He had lost all the pleasures of life that the innocent little Ebenezer had once relished. He missed out on the warmth and comfort of a family and children. He was lost and empty. Mourning the trauma began to allow him to reopen his heart.'[118]

Dickens was writing long before Freud, but with this commitment to Wordsworth's philosophy on childhood development, the idea that hidden trauma should be exposed is not too surprising.

Could we perhaps see Scrooge's redemption as a spiritual one? Dickens was not a religious man, but he did feel Christian teachings were important. When his children began to grow up he wrote a children's book entitled 'The Life Of Our Lord' to neutrally introduce bible stories. He shared a reforming motivation with other religious activists, such as William Booth (the founder of the Salvation Army), and Scrooge's trials leading him to be a pure and loving figure can neatly fit into a biblical narrative. Perhaps it's love that opens Scrooge's heart.

'A Christmas Carol is a tale of redemption. Scrooge is blessed by a series of spiritual

---

[118] Robert Berezin, 'Dickens' Christmas Carol: A Psychiatric Primer of Character and Redemption', accessed 8/19. https://www.madinamerica.com/2017/12/dickens-christmas-carol-character-re-demption/

visitations that enable him to obey the Socratic injunction, "Know yourself," from multiple different spatial and temporal points of view.

Having glimpsed in so short a time the course of his whole life, Scrooge is able, for the first time, to perceive its true trajectory. He realizes that, despite his growing wealth, his greed is alienating everyone around him, making him a boon to no man and a curse to many. Hoping against hope to write a different final chapter, Scrooge embarks on a new life.

In attempting to capture a new spirit of Christmas, Dickens reminds us of the power of the past and the future to change the way we see the present. In confronting Scrooge with the stark contrast between the spirit of generosity in his youth and the isolated, desolate circumstances of his death, Dickens invites readers to contemplate our own life trajectories and begin redrafting our own eulogies while there is still a chance to make changes. Perhaps we, like Scrooge, can rediscover the wonder of an open heart, recognizing that warmth and vitality lie not in the accumulation of wealth but in the dedication of time, talent and treasure to others.'[119]

Redemption was an idea which Dickens firmly and truly believed in, and this can be seen through his tireless work at Urania Cottage, the refuge he helped to create for sex workers who wished to start a new life.

'Over the years Dickens supported many charities and benevolent funds. While he never had much faith in governments, he did have faith in the power of the individual to change for good.'[120]

---

[119] Richard Gunderman, 'How Charles Dickens Redeemed the Spirit of Christmas', accessed 8/19. https://theconversation.com/how-charles-dickens-redeemed-the-spirit-of-christmas-52335

[120] Hartley, Jenny (2008), *Charles Dickens and the House of Fallen Women*, UK: Methuen, 25.

He interviewed each woman extensively and firmly believed that the myth of a 'fallen woman' did not equate to fixed destiny. This was a controversial move considering his contemporaries were spouting ideas like this one:

'The tendency [of a fallen woman's life] is always downward...Even in thieves, there may be an advance. . . But in the present case, rising is a thing unknown. It cannot be. It is all descent.'[121]

This firm belief that redemption was not just a fiction that applied to Scrooge, but actually could be possible for anyone is a key part of Dickens' personality present in A Christmas Carol.

That said, the quickness of Scrooge's conversion is still shocking.

'Modern readers may have trouble with the suddenness of Scrooge's conversion, the readiness with which he gets affectionate and tearful over visions of his younger self. Certainly, his change of heart is not handled with the minutely gradated subtlety we might expect from a modern literary writer, or even from other Victorian novelists such as George Eliot. Determined apologists for Dickens's craftsmanship might argue that we shouldn't underestimate how dramatic an impact it would have on a person to be transported physically back into the past, rather than merely recalling it at a distance. But such a defence would miss the point. Scrooge's conversion is unconvincing, if we subject him to rigorous psychological analysis. However, like many of Dickens's characters, Scrooge refuses to behave according to the rules of literary taste - and that's part of his appeal.

---

[121] Ralph Wardlaw, 'Lectures on Female Prostitution', accessed 8/19. https://archive.org/details/lecturesonfemale00ward/page/n6

A Christmas Carol is an extravagantly symbolic thing - as rich in symbols as Christmas pudding is rich in raisins. Dickens misses no opportunity to cram his thematic concerns into the bodies and utterances of his characters. We are not in the world of Henry James or Alice Munro here, we are in the world of John Bunyan and medieval passion plays, and the sooner we accept this, the better we will enjoy the ride. A Christmas Carol is not a study of one person's emotional and intellectual development, it's a knockabout battle between absolute qualities, dressed up in bizarre forms for maximum thrills. Indeed, when we first meet Ebenezer, he seems an almost supernatural force: "External heat and cold had little influence on Scrooge. No warmth could warm, no wintry weather chill him. No wind that blew was bitterer than he, no falling snow was more intent upon its purpose . . ." With such paranormal credentials, Scrooge plainly needs to be taught the lesson that he's human after all.

Just as moralist writers in the Middle Ages were unselfconscious about bringing on a skeleton wielding a scythe, Dickens is bold enough to devise outrageously obvious - yet poignantly effective - visual metaphors for the way avarice weighs down the soul. Marley's ghost drags a chain made of cash-boxes, keys, padlocks, ledgers, deeds and steel purses. The sky outside is filled with phantoms, all similarly chained, some linked in groups ("they might be guilty governments", proposes Dickens). All are tortured by A Christmas Carol's highly idiosyncratic interpretation of hell: no longer having the power to aid one's fellow mortals. We are shown the old ghost in the white waistcoat, "with a monstrous iron safe attached to its ankle, who cried piteously at being unable to assist a wretched woman with an infant, whom it saw below, upon a doorstep". We swallow the idea that the cap which obscures the divine light streaming from the Ghost of Christmas Past is made of ignoble human passions. We hear the Ghost of Christmas Present proclaiming that he has more than 1,800 brothers, and understand that these represent the years since Christ's birth. In today's literary climate, the symbolism of a writer like DH Lawrence can seem tiresomely heavy-handed, yet Dickens's symbolism, which is a good deal less subtle, somehow gets away with it. It's deranged, fabulous confidence pulls it through.'[122]

We know as soon as we see the cover emblazoned with the name Charles Dickens that there will be moments of unreality: Great Expectations features Miss Havisham in the crumbling, rat infested remains of her wedding reception, David Copperfield has children labelled with their behavioural problems and Pickwick Papers shares poetry dedicated to dead frogs. The worlds that Dickens creates are a little like ours but not completely, so why shouldn't we believe that a man be redeemed overnight through a ghostly epiphany? It seems like a comparatively small leap of faith needed to enjoy this 'little book', as Dickens called it.

[122] Faber, 'Spectral Pleasures'.

Conclusion

Back in 2011, I was teaching English to an almost-fluent class of seventeen year old Chinese students. It was Christmas Eve and I needed to do something challenging, so I showed a clip of The Muppet Christmas Carol and asked them to reconstruct the story or predict what would happen next.

The room erupted.

"We know this story! The Three Christmas Ghosts!"

Okay, I thought. Let's take the challenge up a level. I asked them to write their own version of a story where a character is visited by a ghost and learns something. The story that emerged was fabulous: the headteacher of Number Three Boys School had to experience an evening in their dormitory, including a cold shower, terrible food and, apparently, a roommate with gastric distress.

The original story of a Christmas Carol has transcended its context and become a part of Christmases around the world. The redemption of a 'mean man' through walking in someone else's shoes is universal. I've never been a great lover of Christmas (through a combination of a small family and perpetual disappointment as a child in never getting a white Christmas), but the redemption and social realisation is compelling. I would watch a movie where a racist politician watched an immigrant family's Christmas, or a CEO watches an employee on minimum wage. We could all do with being more socially responsible, and that is the power of this book.

As a native Londoner, I find the context fascinating as it's what Dickens saw in my hometown, and what's still there now. He had power of observation, and hope, and motivation, and that is the magic of the context.

Appendix: 'The Story of the Goblins who stole a Sexton' from 'The Pickwick Papers'

This is widely held to be a prototype of A Christmas Carol, appearing as a chapter in Dickens' first novel.

'In an old abbey town, down in this part of the country, a long, long while ago—so long, that the story must be a true one, because our great-grandfathers implicitly believed it—there officiated as sexton and grave-digger in the churchyard, one Gabriel Grub. It by no means follows that because a man is a sexton, and constantly surrounded by the emblems of mortality, therefore he should be a morose and melancholy man; your undertakers are the merriest fellows in the world; and I once had the honour of being on intimate terms with a mute, who in private life, and off duty, was as comical and jocose a little fellow as ever chirped out a devil-may-care song, without a hitch in his memory, or drained off a good stiff glass without stopping for breath. But notwithstanding these precedents to the contrary, Gabriel Grub was an ill-conditioned, cross-grained, surly fellow—a morose and lonely man, who consorted with nobody but himself, and an old wicker bottle which fitted into his large deep waistcoat pocket—and who eyed each merry face, as it passed him by, with such a deep scowl of malice and ill-humour, as it was difficult to meet without feeling something the worse for.

'A little before twilight, one Christmas Eve, Gabriel shouldered his spade, lighted his lantern, and betook himself towards the old churchyard; for he had got a grave to finish by next morning, and, feeling very low, he thought it might raise his spirits, perhaps, if he went on with his work at once. As he went his way, up the ancient street, he saw the cheerful light of the blazing fires gleam through the old casements, and heard the loud laugh and the cheerful shouts of those who were assembled *around them; he marked the bustling preparations for next day's cheer, and smelled the numerous savoury odours consequent thereupon, as they steamed up from the kitchen windows in clouds. All this was gall and wormwood to the heart of Gabriel Grub; and when groups of children bounded out of the houses, tripped across the road, and were met, before they could knock at the opposite door, by half a dozen curly-headed little rascals who crowded round them as they flocked upstairs to spend the evening in their Christmas games, Gabriel smiled grimly, and clutched the handle of his spade with a firmer grasp, as he thought of measles, scarlet fever, thrush, whooping-cough, and a good many other sources of consolation besides.*

'In this happy frame of mind, Gabriel strode along, returning a short, sullen growl to the good-humoured greetings of such of his neighbours as now and then passed him, until he turned into the dark lane which led to the churchyard. Now, Gabriel had been looking forward to reaching the dark lane, because it was, generally speaking, a nice, gloomy, mournful place, into which the townspeople did not much care to go, except in broad daylight, and when the sun was shining; consequently, he was not a little indignant to hear a young urchin roaring out some jolly song about a merry Christmas, in this very sanctuary which had been called Coffin Lane ever since the days of the old abbey, and the time of the shaven-headed monks. As Gabriel walked on, and the voice drew nearer, he found it proceeded from a small boy, who was hurrying along, to join one of the little parties in the old street, and who, partly to keep himself company, and partly to prepare himself for the occasion, was shouting out the song at the highest pitch of his lungs. So Gabriel waited until the boy came up, and then dodged him into a corner, and rapped him over the head with his lantern five or six times, just to teach him to modulate his voice. And as the boy hurried away with his hand to his head, singing quite a different sort of tune, Gabriel Grub chuckled very heartily to himself, and entered the churchyard, locking the gate behind him.

'He took off his coat, set down his lantern, and getting into the unfinished grave,
112

worked at it for an hour or so with right good-will. But the earth was hardened with the frost, and it was no very easy matter to break it up, and shovel it out; and although there was a moon, it was a very young one, and shed little light upon the grave, which was in the shadow of the church. At any other time, these obstacles would have made Gabriel Grub very moody and miserable, but he was so well pleased with having stopped the small boy's singing, that he took little heed of the scanty progress he had made, and looked down into the grave, when he had finished work for the night, with grim satisfaction, murmuring as he gathered up his things —

Brave lodgings for one, brave lodgings for one,

A few feet of cold earth, when life is done;

A stone at the head, a stone at the feet,

A rich, juicy meal for the worms to eat;

Rank grass overhead, and damp clay around,

Brave lodgings for one, these, in holy ground!

'"Ho! ho!" laughed Gabriel Grub, as he sat himself down on a flat tombstone which was a favourite resting-place of his, and drew forth his wicker bottle. "A coffin at Christmas! A Christmas box! Ho! ho! ho!"

'"Ho! ho! ho!" repeated a voice which sounded close behind him.

'Gabriel paused, in some alarm, in the act of raising the wicker bottle to his lips, and looked round. The bottom of the oldest grave about him was not more still and quiet than the churchyard in the pale moonlight. The cold hoar frost glistened on the tombstones, and sparkled like rows of gems, among the stone carvings of the old church. The snow lay hard and crisp upon the ground; and spread over the thickly-strewn mounds of earth, so white and smooth a cover that it seemed as if corpses lay there, hidden only by their winding sheets. Not the faintest rustle broke the profound tranquillity of the solemn scene. Sound itself appeared to be frozen up, all was so cold and still.

113

'"It was the echoes," said Gabriel Grub, raising the bottle to his lips again.

'"It was not," said a deep voice.

'Gabriel started up, and stood rooted to the spot with astonishment and terror; for his eyes rested on a form that made his blood run cold.

'Seated on an upright tombstone, close to him, was a strange, unearthly figure, whom Gabriel felt at once, was no being of this world. His long, fantastic legs which might have reached the ground, were cocked up, and crossed after a quaint, fantastic fashion; his sinewy arms were bare; and his hands rested on his knees. On his short, round body, he wore a close covering, ornamented with small slashes; a short cloak dangled at his back; the collar was cut into curious peaks, which served the goblin in lieu of ruff or neckerchief; and his shoes curled up at his toes into long points. On his head, he wore a broad-brimmed sugar-loaf hat, garnished with a single feather. The hat was covered with the white frost; and the goblin looked as if he had sat on the same tombstone very comfortably, for two or three hundred years. He was sitting perfectly still; his tongue was put out, as if in derision; and he was grinning at Gabriel Grub with such a grin as only a goblin could call up.

'"It was not the echoes," said the goblin.

'Gabriel Grub was paralysed, and could make no reply.

'"What do you do here on Christmas Eve?" said the goblin sternly.

'"I came to dig a grave, Sir," stammered Gabriel Grub.

'"What man wanders among graves and churchyards on such a night as this?" cried the goblin.

'"Gabriel Grub! Gabriel Grub!" screamed a wild chorus of voices that seemed to fill the churchyard. Gabriel looked fearfully round—nothing was to be seen.

'"What have you got in that bottle?" said the goblin.

'"Hollands, sir," replied the sexton, trembling more than ever; for he had bought it of the smugglers, and he thought that perhaps his questioner might be in the excise department of the goblins.

'"Who drinks Hollands alone, and in a churchyard, on such a night as this?" said the goblin.

'"Gabriel Grub! Gabriel Grub!" exclaimed the wild voices again.

'The goblin leered maliciously at the terrified sexton, and then raising his voice, exclaimed—

'"And who, then, is our fair and lawful prize?"

'To this inquiry the invisible chorus replied, in a strain that sounded like the voices of many choristers singing to the mighty swell of the old church organ—a strain that seemed borne to the sexton's ears upon a wild wind, and to die away as it passed onward; but the burden of the reply was still the same, "Gabriel Grub! Gabriel Grub!"

'The goblin grinned a broader grin than before, as he said, "Well, Gabriel, what do you say to this?"

'The sexton gasped for breath.

'"What do you think of this, Gabriel?" said the goblin, kicking up his feet in the air on either side of the tombstone, and looking at the turned-up points with as much complacency as if he had been contemplating the most fashionable pair of Wellingtons in all Bond Street.

'"It's—it's—very curious, Sir," replied the sexton, half dead with fright; "very curious, and very pretty, but I think I'll go back and finish my work, Sir, if you please."

'"Work!" said the goblin, "what work?"

'"The grave, Sir; making the grave," stammered the sexton.

'"Oh, the grave, eh?" said the goblin; "who makes graves at a time when all other men are merry, and takes a pleasure in it?"

'Again the mysterious voices replied, "Gabriel Grub! Gabriel Grub!"

'"I am afraid my friends want you, Gabriel," said the goblin, thrusting his tongue farther into his cheek than ever—and a most astonishing tongue it was—"I'm afraid my friends want you, Gabriel," said the goblin.

'"Under favour, Sir," replied the horror-stricken sexton, "I don't think they can, Sir; they don't know me, Sir; I don't think the gentlemen have ever seen me, Sir."

'"Oh, yes, they have," replied the goblin; "we know the man with the sulky face and grim scowl, that came down the street to-night, throwing his evil looks at the children, and grasping his burying-spade the tighter. We know the man who struck the boy in the envious malice of his heart, because the boy could be merry, and he could not. We know him, we know him."

'Here, the goblin gave a loud, shrill laugh, which the echoes returned twentyfold; and throwing his legs up in the air, stood upon his head, or rather upon the very point of his sugar-loaf hat, on the narrow edge of the tombstone, whence he threw a Somerset with extraordinary agility, right to the sexton's feet, at which he planted himself in the attitude in which tailors generally sit upon the shop-board.

'"I—I—am afraid I must leave you, Sir," said the sexton, making an effort to move.

'"Leave us!" said the goblin, "Gabriel Grub going to leave us. Ho! ho! ho!"

'As the goblin laughed, the sexton observed, for one instant, a brilliant illumination within the windows of the church, as if the whole building were lighted up; it disappeared, the organ pealed forth a lively air, and whole troops of goblins, the very counterpart of the first one, poured into the churchyard, and began playing at leapfrog with the tombstones, never stopping for an instant to take breath, but "overing" the highest among them, one after the other, with the most marvellous dexterity. The first goblin was a most astonishing leaper, and none of the others could come near him; even in the extremity of his terror the sexton could not help observing, that while *his friends were content to leap over the common-sized gravestones, the first one took the family vaults, iron railings and all, with as much ease as if they had been so many street-posts.*

'At last the game reached to a most exciting pitch; the organ played quicker and quicker, and the goblins leaped faster and faster, coiling themselves up, rolling head over heels upon the ground, and bounding over the tombstones like footballs. The sexton's brain whirled round with the rapidity of the motion he beheld, and his legs reeled beneath him, as the spirits flew before his eyes; when the goblin king, suddenly darting towards him, laid his hand upon his collar, and sank with him through the earth.

'When Gabriel Grub had had time to fetch his breath, which the rapidity of his descent had for the moment taken away, he found himself in what appeared to be a large cavern, surrounded on all sides by crowds of goblins, ugly and grim; in the centre of the room, on an elevated seat, was stationed his friend of the churchyard; and close behind him stood Gabriel Grub himself, without power of motion.

'"Cold to-night," said the king of the goblins, "very cold. A glass of something warm here!"

'At this command, half a dozen officious goblins, with a perpetual smile upon their faces, whom Gabriel Grub imagined to be courtiers, on that account, hastily disappeared, and presently returned with a goblet of liquid fire, which they presented to the king.

'"Ah!" cried the goblin, whose cheeks and throat were transparent, as he tossed down the flame, "this warms one, indeed! Bring a bumper of the same, for Mr. Grub."

'It was in vain for the unfortunate sexton to protest that he was not in the habit of taking anything warm at night; one of the goblins held him while another poured the

117

blazing liquid down his throat; the whole assembly screeched with laughter, as he coughed and choked, and wiped away the tears which gushed plentifully from his eyes, after swallowing the burning draught.

'"And now," said the king, fantastically poking the taper corner of his sugar-loaf hat into the sexton's eye, and thereby occasioning him the most exquisite pain; "and now, show the man of misery and gloom, a few of the pictures from our own great storehouse!"

'As the goblin said this, a thick cloud which obscured the remoter end of the cavern rolled gradually away, and disclosed, apparently at a great distance, a small and scantily furnished, but neat and clean apartment. A crowd of little children were gathered round a bright fire, clinging to their mother's gown, and gambolling around her chair. The mother occasionally rose, and drew aside the window-curtain, as if to look for some expected object; a frugal meal was ready spread upon the table; and an elbow chair was placed near the fire. A knock was heard at the door; the mother opened it, and the children crowded round her, and clapped their hands for joy, as their father entered. He was wet and weary, and shook the snow from his garments, as the children crowded round him, and seizing his cloak, hat, stick, and gloves, with busy zeal, ran with them from the room. Then, as he sat down to his meal before the fire, the children climbed about his knee, and the mother sat by his side, and all seemed happiness and comfort.

'But a change came upon the view, almost imperceptibly. The scene was altered to a small bedroom, where the fairest and youngest child lay dying; the roses had fled from his cheek, and the light from his eye; and even as the sexton looked upon him with an interest he had never felt or known before, he died. His young brothers and sisters crowded round his little bed, and seized his tiny hand, so cold and heavy; but they shrank back from its touch, and looked with awe on his infant face; for calm and tranquil as it was, and sleeping in rest and peace as the beautiful child seemed to be, they saw that he was dead, and they knew that he was an angel looking down upon, and blessing them, from a bright and happy Heaven.

'Again the light cloud passed across the picture, and again the subject changed. The father and mother were old and helpless now, and the number of those about them was diminished more than half; but content and cheerfulness sat on every face, and beamed in every eye, as they crowded round the fireside, and told and listened to old stories of earlier and bygone days. Slowly and peacefully, the father sank into the grave, and, soon after, the sharer of all his cares and troubles followed him to a place of rest. The few who yet survived them, kneeled by their tomb, and watered the green turf which covered it with their tears; then rose, and turned away, sadly and mournfully, but not with bitter cries, or despairing lamentations, for they knew that they should one day meet again; and once more they mixed with the busy world, and their content and cheerfulness were restored. The cloud settled upon the picture, and concealed it from the sexton's view.

'"What do you think of that?" said the goblin, turning his large face towards Gabriel Grub.

'Gabriel murmured out something about its being very pretty, and looked somewhat ashamed, as the goblin bent his fiery eyes upon him.

'"You a miserable man!" said the goblin, in a tone of excessive contempt. "You!" He appeared disposed to add more, but indignation choked his utterance, so he lifted up one of his very pliable legs, and, flourishing it above his head a little, to insure his aim, administered a good sound kick to Gabriel Grub; immediately after which, all the goblins in waiting crowded round the wretched sexton, and kicked him without mercy, according to the established and invariable custom of courtiers upon earth, who kick whom royalty kicks, and hug whom royalty hugs.

'"Show him some more!" said the king of the goblins.

119

'At these words, the cloud was dispelled, and a rich and beautiful landscape was disclosed to view—there is just such another, to this day, within half a mile of the old abbey town. The sun shone from out the clear blue sky, the water sparkled beneath his rays, and the trees looked greener, and the flowers more gay, beneath its cheering influence. The water rippled on with a pleasant sound, the trees rustled in the light wind that murmured among their leaves, the birds sang upon the boughs, and the lark carolled on high her welcome to the morning. Yes, it was morning; the bright, balmy morning of summer; the minutest leaf, the smallest blade of grass, was instinct with life. The ant crept forth to her daily toil, the butterfly fluttered and basked in the warm rays of the sun; myriads of insects spread their transparent wings, and revelled in their brief but happy existence. Man walked forth, elated with the scene; and all was brightness and splendour.

'"You a miserable man!" said the king of the goblins, in a more contemptuous tone than before. And again the king of the goblins gave his leg a flourish; again it descended on the shoulders of the sexton; and again the attendant goblins imitated the example of their chief.

'Many a time the cloud went and came, and many a lesson it taught to Gabriel Grub, who, although his shoulders smarted with pain from the frequent applications of the goblins' feet thereunto, looked on with an interest that nothing could diminish. He saw that men who worked hard, and earned their scanty bread with lives of labour, were cheerful and happy; and that to the most ignorant, the sweet face of Nature was a never-failing source of cheerfulness and joy. He saw those who had been delicately nurtured, and tenderly brought up, cheerful under privations, and superior to suffering, that would have crushed many of a rougher grain, because they bore within their own bosoms the materials of happiness, contentment, and peace. He saw that women, the tenderest and most fragile of all God's creatures, were the oftenest superior to sorrow, adversity, and distress; and he saw that it was because they bore, *in their own hearts, an inexhaustible well-spring of affection and devotion. Above all, he saw that men like himself, who snarled at the mirth and cheerfulness of others, were the foulest weeds on the fair surface of the earth; and setting all the good of the world against the evil, he came to the conclusion that it was a very decent and respectable sort of world after all. No sooner had he formed it, than the cloud which had closed over the last picture, seemed to settle on his senses, and lull him to repose. One by one, the goblins faded from his sight; and, as the last one disappeared, he sank to sleep.*

'The day had broken when Gabriel Grub awoke, and found himself lying at full length on the flat gravestone in the churchyard, with the wicker bottle lying empty by his side, and his coat, spade, and lantern, all well whitened by the last night's frost, scattered on the ground. The stone on which he had first seen the goblin seated, stood bolt upright before him, and the grave at which he had worked, the night before, was not far off. At first, he began to doubt the reality of his adventures, but the acute pain in his shoulders when he attempted to rise, assured him that the kicking of the goblins was certainly not ideal. He was staggered again, by observing no traces of footsteps in the snow on which the goblins had played at leap-frog with the gravestones, but he speedily accounted for this circumstance when he remembered that, being spirits, they would leave no visible impression behind them. So, Gabriel Grub got on his feet as well as he could, for the pain in his back; and, brushing the frost off his coat, put it on, and turned his face towards the town.

'But he was an altered man, and he could not bear the thought of returning to a place where his repentance would be scoffed at, and his reformation disbelieved. He hesitated for a few moments; and then turned away to wander where he might, and seek his bread elsewhere.

'The lantern, the spade, and the wicker bottle were found, that day, in the churchyard. There were a great many speculations about the sexton's fate, at first, but it was

speedily determined that he had been carried away by the goblins; and there were not wanting some very credible witnesses who had distinctly seen him whisked through the air on the back of a chestnut horse blind of one eye, with the hind-quarters of a lion, and the tail of a bear. At length all this was devoutly believed; and the new sexton used to exhibit to the curious, for a trifling emolument, a good-sized piece of the church weathercock which had been accidentally kicked off by the aforesaid horse in his aerial flight, and picked up by himself in the churchyard, a year or two afterwards.

'Unfortunately, these stories were somewhat disturbed by the unlooked-for reappearance of Gabriel Grub himself, some ten years afterwards, a ragged, contented, rheumatic old man. He told his story to the clergyman, and also to the mayor; and in course of time it began to be received as a matter of history, in which form it has continued down to this very day. The believers in the weathercock tale, having misplaced their confidence once, were not easily prevailed upon to part with it again, so they looked as wise as they could, shrugged their shoulders, touched their foreheads, and murmured something about Gabriel Grub having drunk all the Hollands, and then fallen asleep on the flat tombstone; and they affected to explain what he supposed he had witnessed in the goblin's cavern, by saying that he had seen the world, and grown wiser. But this opinion, which was by no means a popular one at any time, gradually died off; and be the matter how it may, as Gabriel Grub was afflicted with rheumatism to the end of his days, this story has at least one moral, if it teach no better one—and that is, that if a man turn sulky and drink by himself at Christmas time, he may make up his mind to be not a bit the better for it: let the spirits be never so good, or let them be even as many degrees beyond proof, as those which Gabriel Grub saw in the goblin's cavern.'[123]

---

[123] Charles Dickens, 'The Pickwick Papers', accessed 7/19. https://www.gutenberg.org/files/580/580-h/580-h.htm#link2HCH0029

Bibliography

Robert Berezin, 'Dickens' Christmas Carol: A Psychiatric Primer of Character and Redemption', accessed 8/19. https://www.madinamerica.com/2017/12/dickens-christmas-carol-character-redemption/

Jerry Bowyer, 'Mathus and Scrooge: How Charles Dickens Put Holly Branch Through the Heart Of The Worst Economics Ever', accessed 7/19. https://www.forbes.com/sites/jerrybowyer/2012/12/24/malthus-and-scrooge-how-charles-dickens-put-holly-branch-through-the-heart-of-the-worst-economics-ever/#11e92134672d

John Broich, 'The real reason Dickens wrote A Christmas Carol', accessed 8/19. https://time.com/4597964/history-charles-dickens-christmas-carol/

Tracy Chevalier, 'Victorian Morning Etiquette', accessed 7/19. https://www.tchevalier.com/fallingangels/bckgrnd/mourning/

Rupert Christiansen, 'Dickens' Attitude to the Law', accessed 8/19. https://ex-ec.typepad.com/greatexpectations/dickens-attitude-to-the-law.html

Lydia Craig 'Man and Meat: A Christmas Carol's Cannibalistic Menace in Historical Perspective', accessed 8/19. http://dickenssociety.org/?p=1535

Matthew Davis, 'Did Charles Dickens really save poor children and clean up the slums?', accessed 8/19. https://www.bbc.co.uk/news/magazine-16907648

Devito, Carlo (2014), *Inventing Scrooge: The Incredible True Story Behind Dickens' Legendary A Christmas Carol*, Maine: Cider Mill Press.

Charles Dickens, 'Accident and Disaster', accessed 8/19. http://www.d-jo.org.uk/household-narrative-of-current-events/year-1850/page-11.html

Charles Dickens, 'A Christmas Tree', accessed 7/19. http://www.djo.org.uk/household-words/volume-ii/page-289.html

Dickens, Charles (1995 ed), *Christmas Books,* UK: Wordsworth Classics

Charles Dickens, 'Great Expectations', accessed 7/19. https://www.gutenberg.org/files/766/766-h/766-h.htm

Charles Dickens, 'Little Dorrit', accessed 7/19. https://www.gutenberg.org/files/963/963-h/963-h.htm

Charles Dickens 'Sketches by Boz', accessed 7/19. https://ebooks.adelaide.edu.au/d/dickens/charles/d54sb/chapter34.html

Charles Dickens, 'The Old Curiosity Shop', accessed 7/19. https://www.gutenberg.org/files/700/700-h/700-h.htm

Charles Dickens, 'The Pickwick Papers', accessed 7/19. https://www.gutenberg.org/files/580/580-h/580-h.htm#link2HCH0029

Lucinda Dickens Hawksley, 'Charles Dickens and the women who made him', accessed 8/19. https://www.theguardian.com/books/2016/apr/06/charles-dickens-and-the-women-who-made-him

Dickens, Mamie (2011 edition), *My Father as I Recall Him*, USA: Library of Alexandria.

Andrzej Diniejko, 'Charles Dickens as Social Commentator and Critic', accessed 7/19. http://www.victorianweb.org/authors/dickens/diniejko.html

Ian Dooley, 'Charles Dickens Describes a Ragged School to Angela Burdett-Coutts', accessed 8/19. https://blogs.princeton.edu/cotsen/2016/06/the-ragged-school-a-letter-from-charles-dickens-to-angela-burdett-coutts/

Michael Faber, 'Spectral Pleasures', accessed 8/19. https://www.the-guardian.com/books/2005/dec/24/featuresreviews.guardianreview22

Dr Lindsey Fitzharris, 'Death and Childhood in Victorian England', accessed 7/19. http://www.drlindseyfitzharris.com/2013/10/15/death-childhood-in-victo-rian-england/

Flanders, Judith (2017), *Christmas: A Biography*, UK: Picador.

Sarah Flew, 'Unveiling the anonymous philanthropist: charity in the nineteenth century', accessed 8/19. http://eprints.lse.ac.uk/61080/1/Flew_Unveil-ing_the_Anonymous_Philanthropist.pdf

Forster, John (2019 ed), *The Life of Charles Dickens*, UK: Forgotten Books.

John Gregory 'A Father's Legacy to his Daughters', accessed 7/19. https://www.gutenberg.org/files/50108/50108-h/50108-h.htm#conduct

Goodman, Ruth (2013), *How to be a Victorian*, UK: Penguin.

Richard Gunderman, 'How Charles Dickens Redeemed the Spirit of Christmas', accessed 8/19. https://theconversation.com/how-charles-dickens-re-deemed-the-spirit-of-christmas-52335

Hartley, Jenny (2008), *Charles Dickens and the House of Fallen Women*, UK: Methuen.

Charlotte Hodgman, 'The Rise and Fall of the Workhouse', accessed 7/19. https://www.historyextra.com/period/victorian/the-rise-and-fall-of-the-work-house/

Margaret Holborn, 'Charles Dickens dies - archive, June 1870', accessed 8/19. https://uploads.guim.co.uk/2017/06/07/Manchester_-Guardian_15_June_1870_report_of_funeral_of_Charles_Dickens.pdf

Tom Hughes, 'An Announcement from Mr Dickens', accessed 8/19. http://victoriancalendar.blogspot.com/2011/06/june-12-1858.html

Irving, Washington (2014 ed), *Old Christmas*, UK: Aristeus Books.

Ben Johnson 'A Victorian Christmas', accessed 7/19. https://www.historic-uk.com/HistoryUK/HistoryofEngland/A-Victorian-Christmas/

E D H Johnson, 'Dickens and His Readers', accessed 8/19. http://www.victorianweb.org/authors/dickens/edh/3.html

Jordan, John O (ed, 2001), *The Cambridge Companion to Charles Dickens*, UK: Cambridge.

Thomas Laquer, 'Bodies Death and Pauper Funerals', accessed 7/19. https://pdfs.semanticscholar.org/a0f3/be5d5aae6e4cc07ad-d3cf7a96b570533170a.pdf

Lauren Laverne, 'Dickens' Christmas Carol didn't invent the holiday, but it did help revive it', accessed 7/19. https://www.theguardian.com/lifeandstyle/2014/

dec/21/dickens-christmas-carol-didnt-invent-holiday-help-revived-it-lauren-laverne

Donna Loftus, 'The Rise of the Victorian Middle Class', accessed 8/19. https://www.bbc.co.uk/history/british/victorians/middle_classes_01.shtml

Thomas Malthus 'An Essay on the Principle of Population', accessed 7/19. https://www.gutenberg.org/files/4239/4239-h/4239-h.htm

Harriet Marsden, 'Disability History Month: Barnardos publishes 125-year-old photos of disabled children', accessed 7/19. https://www.independent.co.uk/arts-entertainment/photography/disability-history-month-barnardos-photos-disabled-children-kids-differently-abled-handicapped-a8071336.html

Emma Mason, 'Feeling Dickensian Feeling', accessed 8/19. https://www.19.bbk.ac.uk/articles/10.16995/ntn.454/galley/314/download/

VL McBeath, 'Consumption: The Most Feared Of Diseases', accessed 7/19. https://valmcbeath.com/consumption-the-most-feared-of-diseases/

Marilyn A Mendoza, 'Death and Mourning Practices in the Victorian Age', accessed 7/19. https://www.psychologytoday.com/gb/blog/understanding-grief/201812/death-and-mourning-practices-in-the-victorian-age

Norman Miller, 'John Elwes: scrimper who inspired Ebeneezer Scrooge', accessed 7/19. https://www.telegraph.co.uk/only-in-britain/man-who-inspired-ebenezer-scrooge/

Ross Ogden and Daniel Beltran, 'Infant and Child Mortality', accessed 7/19. https://londonspulse.org/2016/05/02/infantandchildmortality/

John O'Neill, 'A Christmas Carol is not a secular tale', accessed 8/19. https://eu.detroitnews.com/story/opinion/2014/12/25/christmas-carol-secular/20887623/

Frank Prochaska, 'Women and philanthropy in nineteenth century England', accessed 8/19. http://www.philanthropy-impact.org/article/women-and-philanthropy-19th-century-england

Pykett, Lyn (2002), *Critical Issues: Charles Dickens*, UK: Palgrave.

Nicola Slawson, 'Charles Dickens' A Christmas Carol' inspired by visits to Cornwall', accessed 7/19. https://www.theguardian.com/books/2017/dec/19/charles-dickens-a-christmas-carol-inspired-by-visits-to-cornwall

Michael Stern, 'Like Being Buried Alive: Charles Dickens on Solitary Confinement in American Prisons', accessed 8/19. https://prospect.org/article/being-%e2%80%9cburied-alive%e2%80%9d-charles-dickens-solitary-confinement-america%e2%80%99s-prisons

Allyson Thaxton, 'Married to Money: Dowries in Victorian England', accessed 8/19. https://byuprideandprejudice.wordpress.com/2014/02/03/married-to-money-dowries-in-victorian-england/

Tomalin, Claire (2011), *Charles Dickens: A Life,* UK: Penguin.

Tomalin, Claire (1990), *The Invisible Woman: The Story of Nellie Ternan and Charles Dickens*, UK: Penguin.

Unknown, 'Dickens and the Victorian City', accessed 8/19. http://dickens.port.ac.uk/education/

Unknown, 'History of Christmas', accessed 7/19. http://www.bbc.co.uk/victorianchristmas/history.shtml

Unknown, 'Revealed: the Scot who inspired Dickens' Scrooge', accessed 7/19. https://www.scotsman.com/news-2-15012/revealed-the-scot-who-inspired-dickens-scrooge-1-571985

Unknown, 'Rickets', accessed 7/19. http://broughttolife.sciencemuseum.org.uk/broughttolife/techniques/rickets

Unknown, 'What were Charles Dickens' views toward religion?', accessed 7/19. https://dickens.ucsc.edu/resources/faq/religion.html

Ralph Wardlaw, 'Lectures on Female Prostitution', accessed 8/19. https://archive.org/details/lecturesonfemale00ward/page/n6

Edmund Wilson, 'The Two Scrooges', accessed 7/19. https://newrepublic.com/article/100447/the-two-scrooges

Emily Witt, 'Daddy Issues: On the Worthless Brood of Charles Dickens', accessed 8/19. https://observer.com/2012/12/daddy-issues-on-the-worthless-brood-of-charles-dickens/

Robert Wright 'How Charles Dickens rebukes 'overpopulation' fear mongers like Scrooge, Malthus and even today's environmentalists', accessed 7/19. https://business.financialpost.com/opinion/how-charles-dickens-rebukes-overpopulation-fearmongers-like-scrooge-malthus-and-even-todays-environmentalists

Printed in Great Britain
by Amazon